# SENATE AND PROVINCES

## 78–49 B.C.

# SENATE & PROVINCES

## 78–49 B.C.

*Some aspects of the foreign policy
and provincial relations of the Senate
during the closing years of the
Roman Republic*

by

## J. MACDONALD COBBAN

*Sometime Scholar of Jesus College, Cambridge
Assistant Master at King Edward VI School,
Southampton*

THIRLWALL PRIZE ESSAY 1935

CAMBRIDGE
AT THE UNIVERSITY PRESS
1935

TO

MY FATHER AND MOTHER

# CONTENTS

*Author's Note*                                    *page* ix

*Introduction*                                          xi

*Chapter* I.  The Sullan Restoration                     1

    II.  The Foreign Policy of the Senate        39

    III.  The Appointment of the Provincial
        Governor                                71

    IV.  Lucullus and Pompey                     99

    V.  The Administration of the Provinces      138

    VI.  Roman Rule in Practice                  186

*Bibliography*                                          208

*Index*                                                 211

# AUTHOR'S NOTE

THIS essay was conceived and partly executed during my tenure of the Sandys Studentship in the year 1932–1933: it has been completed in the leisure hours of the past eighteen months.

In dealing with such a familiar period of history as the closing years of the Roman Republic, it is difficult not to trespass on ground already covered by others. As far as possible I have endeavoured to trace my material back to original sources, but I am fully conscious of the debt I owe to previous students in the same field. The works from which I have derived especial help are distinguished in the bibliography.

It would be ungracious not to acknowledge here the many kindnesses I received at the University of Vienna, where I spent six months of research work: I shall not easily forget the helpful courtesy of Professor Wilhelm and Professor Egger. I am grateful also to the British School at Rome for its hospitality; to the University College of Southampton for the library facilities afforded me during the past year; and to my present Headmaster, Mr Clifford Harper, who willingly allowed me to postpone taking up my appointment until after the completion of my studentship. To Mr G. H. Stevenson, of University College, Oxford, I am indebted for many helpful criticisms and suggestions. Above all, I would thank Professor F. E. Adcock, of King's College, Cambridge, without whose constant advice and encouragement this essay would never have been written.

As one who has had little experience of preparing manuscript for publication, I would pay tribute to the work of the Cambridge University Press. The vigilance of its readers has done much to lighten the task of revision: whatever errors of omission and commission remain are mine alone.

The usual abbreviations are employed for references to classical authors. In the case of Cicero, reference is made to the work alone. Modern works listed in the bibliography which have already been cited in text or foot-note are referred to by the name of the author and the abbreviation *op. cit.*, except where this would cause ambiguity.

The initials *C.A.H.* refer to the *Cambridge Ancient History*.

J. MACDONALD COBBAN

*August* 1935
*Scunthorpe, Lincs.*

# INTRODUCTION

THE THIRTY YEARS from 80 to 50 B.C. comprise one of the most interesting periods of Roman history. The constitutional problems which are worked out in it are of first-rate importance, while the personal drama of the triumvirs can still stir our passions. 'Public life in Rome had a man-to-man attitude':[1] and the history of the time is dominated by the rivalry and ambitions of Caesar, Pompey, Crassus and Cicero. But behind the protagonists of the drama stands the Senate, and it too had no mean part to play. All the time the Triumvirs were manœuvring for power at Rome the Senate was carrying on the government at home and abroad. The unrest at Rome could not fail to have its repercussions elsewhere, and the political changes in the capital had a far-reaching effect on the government of the provinces. The Senate, as restored by Sulla, was faced with an extraordinarily difficult task, and in the end it proved unequal to it; but it did not succumb without a struggle, and even in its fall it provided many examples of those old virtues by which it had risen to power in the first place.

The object of this essay is to discuss the position of the Senate under the Sullan régime, and the factors which influenced its policy as an imperial power. The appointment of the provincial governor raises questions of importance, while the control exerted by the Senate

[1] J. Petersson, *Cicero; a Biography*. Cf. Gelzer, *Die Nobilität der römischen Republik*, p. 114: 'Seit dem hannibalischen Krieg wiest das politische Leben unleugbar einen starken individualistischen Zug auf.'

over its deputies is briefly outlined. The career of Lucullus and his command in the East perhaps receives disproportionate attention: but this can be justified by the fact that he is one of the few representatives of the Senate of whom we can draw a full-length picture. He personified in himself the virtues and vices of the restored oligarchy; his relations with Pompey and the Equites throw considerable light on the political cross-currents of the day; and his downfall symbolised and foreshadowed the downfall of the Senate. Finally some attempt is made to assess the position of the provincials, and the benefits they received from Roman rule.

The history of the last half-century of the Republic has been so fully worked over by modern scholars that this essay has little claim to originality. Its aim is, not to add to the detailed knowledge of the period, but to discuss one aspect of it which has received too little attention—the position of the Senate, especially in relation to the provinces and dependencies of Rome.

# THE SULLAN RESTORATION

## SULLA'S REFORM OF THE SENATE

WHEN SULLA became Dictator in 81 B.C. he carried through a series of laws of far-reaching importance. The keystone of these reforms was the restoration of the Senate. This was not merely an attempt to patch up a crumbling edifice, for Sulla was no Die-hard Tory, but a far-seeing administrator; and with Schur[1] we can see in his reform and reconstitution of the Senate a 'great example of conservative progress'. By the degradation of the tribunate, and the restoration of the jury-courts, the Senate was firmly established as the sovereign body in the State, but it was a Senate far different from that of the previous century. No longer was its composition to depend on the arbitrary will of the Censor. The *cursus honorum* was strictly regulated, and all quaestors were to enter the Senate automatically after their year of office. This meant that the Senate was continually being strengthened by the influx of new blood. It became a body of experienced ex-magistrates, and in so far as the election to office still rested on the popular vote the appointment of the Senate was ultimately dependent on the people. By this means Sulla avoided the two extremes; the Senate did not become a narrow and self-chosen council of oligarchs, nor, since they were elected for life, were its members compelled to set their sails to the

[1] W. Schur, 'Homo Novus', *Bonn Jahrb.* 1929, p. 54.

passing breeze of popular opinion. The depleted ranks of the restored Senate were filled up by the immediate appointment of three hundred new members; these were recruited in the main from the ranks of the Equites, a fact which must have had some effect on the politics of the next thirty years.[1]

Sulla has rather cruelly been styled a 'master-builder upon sand', but it was not his foundations that were at fault. His structure fell as the result of external forces, the ambition of the military commanders, and the growing pressure of the Equites and the people. It is easy to misjudge Sulla in the light of after-events; but to an impartial observer in the year 80 the Sullan system would have appeared as aristocracy at its best. Sulla had checked the dangers of demagogic action, and he had consolidated the Senate on a wider and more popular basis. Schur points out the similarity between the aims of Sulla and Drusus; but Sulla had that genius for organisation which his predecessor had so conspicuously lacked. It is noteworthy that Cicero, who was far from being a reactionary, expresses his admiration for the Sullan Senate.[2] It was only later historians who saw in it a stillborn failure.

Sulla's motives in thus re-establishing the Senate have been variously explained. His abdication at the height of his power and his refusal to set up a tyranny presented an insoluble problem even to the men of his generation. It is indeed difficult to believe that he acted from sheer altruism. More probably he was frankly tired of public

---

[1] The actual date of this addition is uncertain. It is discussed at length by E. G. Hardy in the *Journal of Roman Studies*, 1916, p. 59.

[2] *de legibus*, III, 12, 27.

life; this apathy was, as we shall see, no uncommon trait in Roman politics. Yet he was by instinct and training a bureaucrat, and his natural desire for efficiency would not let him abandon the State to stumble along in its old haphazard way. His own experiences had taught him that the government of a great empire could not be left to the caprices of a popular assembly. Since the principle of representation was scarcely known in the ancient world, the alternatives were tyranny and oligarchy. He was unwilling to incur the onus of the former; the existing Senate, purged as it was by the ruthless proscriptions, provided an excellent basis for the establishment of the latter. Even Ferrero, who scathingly dismisses Sulla's reforms as mere 'police-work',[1] admits that he was 'a sincere republican'. The man whose attempt to conserve and strengthen an old form of government ends in failure is rarely appreciated at his true worth. The military monarchy was perhaps inevitable, but Sulla, like Metternich, gave a war-sick world an invaluable respite; and like Metternich, he has been depicted as the heartless cynic who deliberately attempts to buttress up a system which he knows to be rotten.

Carcopino[2] has recently propounded a new view of Sulla. He sees in his reforms a deliberate attempt to establish his own monarchy; it was only an alliance between Pompey and the nobles which led him to retire rather than risk a very doubtful conflict. The thesis is interesting but the evidence is unconvincing. Carcopino neglects or minimises what is inconsistent with his theory, as for instance Sulla's abolition of the cheap corn

[1] Ferrero, *The Greatness and Decline of Rome* (Eng. trans. I, 116.)
[2] J. Carcopino, *Sylla, ou la monarchie manquée.*

system, and attaches exaggerated importance to such
incidents as his assumption of the name of Felix, and his
appropriation of royal privileges. The French savant's
conclusion that 'Sulla's famous system was only an
asphyxiant for the nobles'[1] is directly contrary to the
facts. However we interpret his motives, the result of
his reforms is clear. It was to re-establish the rule of
the senatorial oligarchy. On laying aside his office Sulla
is reported to have said 'I have lifted the Senate into the
saddle; let us see if it can ride'; and this may well represent the attitude with which he retired into private life.

## PROCEDURE IN THE SENATE

The restored Senate was largely responsible for the
government of the Roman world. From Cicero's letters
and other sources we can gather a fair idea of the manner
in which it handled its trust; and there is enough evidence to prove that its 'inefficiency' has been greatly
exaggerated in the past. It is true that occasionally an
incompetent magistrate showed himself ignorant of his
duties,[2] but the president of the day usually conducted
business methodically and with despatch. Formal divisions of the Senate, with their accompanying delay,
seem to have been rare. Perhaps it was only when both
sides were about equal that the house divided. It is noteworthy that in moments of emergency the usual rules of
procedure could be relaxed or modified.[3]

[1] *Op. cit.* p. 77.

[2] E.g. Laterensis the praetor, whose mistakes are exposed by Caelius
in *ad fam.* VIII, 8, 3—*leges ignorans*.

[3] An instance occurred during the debate on the punishment of the
Catilinarian conspirators. It was the consul-elect, Silanus, who first
proposed the death sentence; but Cicero, contrary to custom, chose to

There are two specific charges which are frequently brought against the Senate.

A. It has been suggested that the normal attendance in the Senate was very poor. There was no fixed quorum as a general rule, but the house could be counted out on the demand either of the president or of a private member.[1] Cicero's letters furnish us with instances where business had to be postponed in the absence of a large enough house. In 51 the consul Marcellus was twice foiled in this way in his attempts to have Caesar recalled.[2] On the other hand, business could be facilitated by neglecting to demand a count, and hence decrees could be rushed through in a small house.[3]

Yet this evidence must not be overstressed. It is true that in the year 57 a house of two hundred was greeted by Cicero as being 'fuller than we could have expected in the month of December towards the holidays', but at such a period the attendance naturally sank very low. On the other hand, Cicero mentions a house of 415 in 61 while four years later no less than 416 senators voted in favour of his recall from exile. Curio's final motion in the Senate, at the close of 50, that both Caesar and Pompey should resign their commands, was passed by

put to the vote the motion of Cato, who was merely tribune-elect, because it was his speech which had rallied the wavering conservatives. Moreover, his downright expression of opinion was admirably suited for adoption as the strong substantive motion which Cicero required (*ad Att.* xii, 21, 1).

(For a discussion of the procedure of the Senate, see A. H. J. Greenidge, *Roman Public Life.*)

[1] Willems, *Le Sénat de la République romaine.* A quorum of 200 was established by Cornelius in 66 for a special purpose (the granting of dispensations), but this was probably intended to be a nominal minimum.

[2] *ad fam.* viii, 5, 3; 9, 2.　　　　[3] *ad Att.* x, 4, 9: *surrepto.*

a majority of 370 to 22.[1] It is probable that the average attendance of the Senate was considerably above that of our own Upper House, the efficiency of which is admitted even by its opponents.[2] Cicero directly asserts that it is the duty of a good senator to be regular in his attendance at the Senate-house.[3] The senators were not paid deputies, but public-spirited ex-magistrates, in many cases in the evening of their lives. In addition to their deliberative duties they furnished one panel of the juries. Hence it was impossible for them to attend every meeting of the Senate; but it does seem that in moments of crisis they were to be found in their places in the house.

B. The Senate has also been accused of a lack of expedition in the transaction of business. Groebe[4] has collected a formidable list of instances where a measure was obstructed or talked out. This method was first adopted by the father of Verres in 72 to prevent an awkward inquiry into the conduct of his son. It was raised to a fine art by Cato, and that staunch constitutionalist Cicero recommended it as a rare expedient.[5] It could indeed serve a useful purpose, but in the hands of such an unscrupulous politician as Clodius it became a dangerous tool; particularly when he strengthened his position by bringing up his street-gang to the Senate-

[1] *ad Q.F.* ii, 1, 1; *ad. Att.* i, 14, 5; *post red. ad sen.* 10, 26; Appian, *b.c.* ii, 30.

[2] For the sake of comparison we may note that one of the highest figures reached in a division in the House of Lords since the War was on December 14, 1927, when the Second Reading of the Revised Prayer Book Measure was carried by 241 votes to 88.

[3] *de dom.* 4, 8.

[4] 'Die Obstruktion im römischen Senat', *Klio*, v, 229.

[5] *II in Verr.* ii, 39, 96; *de leg.* iii, 18, 40.

house.[1] Usually, however, the strong common-sense of the Senate prevented matters from reaching an impasse, and the majority of the house either yielded to the intransigeance of the opposition or came to some understanding with it. Thus in 50, when C. Lucilius Hirrus was proposing to block a *supplicatio* in honour of Cicero, Caelius saw him privately and persuaded him to withdraw his opposition.[2] A rare instance of the use of actual violence was provided by Caesar in 59, when he forcibly prevented Cato from blocking his Agrarian Law.

Obstruction by a member of the house was in fact a legitimate piece of parliamentary tactics, such as has not been unknown in our own time.[3] Less defensible was the method of obstructing business by the intervention of a tribune. This ancient office was now used merely for political ends, and the popular leaders found that a friendly tribune could easily block unwelcome proposals in the Senate by his official veto. This manœuvre was seen at its worst during the controversy over the provincial appointments in 51–50. It must be admitted that the misuse of the tribunicial veto during the closing decade of the Republic was one of the most discreditable chapters in Roman history. Nor can the Senate be entirely absolved from responsibility for this. Sulla, foreseeing this danger, had limited the veto of the tribunes

[1] *ad Q.F.* ii, 1, 3: *Tum Clodius rogatus diem dicendo eximere coepit....* *Eius operae repente clamorem sustulerunt.*

[2] *ad fam.* viii, 11, 2.

[3] *The Times* of February 7, 1933, quotes some interesting examples of the use of this manœuvre in the U.S.A. Senate. In 1908 the elder Lafollette made a record by speaking for eighteen hours against the Aldrich-Freeland Currency Bill. Even our own Irish members, in the old House of Commons, did not show such endurance.

to its old function of affording protection to individual sufferers. By permitting the restoration of the tribunicial powers so that the veto could once more be exercised in public affairs the Senate was preparing for its own degradation.

## PARTIES IN THE SENATE

The historians of the nineteenth century tended to view the Senate in the light of contemporary politics, and postulated definite parties with fixed aims and programmes. This view has been exploded by more recent students,[1] and it is now established that there never existed a party system, as we know it, in ancient Rome.

In the first place, political parties are based not so much on a difference of opinion between the leaders as on a deep-rooted cleavage of the people. Now the Roman people was not politically self-conscious. It would vote for the popular demagogue of the moment in the Comitia, but it had no fixed principles beyond a determination to secure the maximum amount of government subsidy. To speak of a 'democratic' party in our sense, under the leadership of Crassus or Caesar, is misleading. The line of division in Rome was not vertical but horizontal, and lay between the rich and the poor. The popular leaders who sought to exploit the needs of the poor did so for their own ends, and not through any genuine attachment to democratic principles.

Secondly, the corporate sense of the Roman nobility prevented the growth of any hard and fast parties. The

[1] E.g. F. Münzer and M. Gelzer (see bibliography; also reviews by Gelzer, *N. Jahrb.* 1920, p. 440, and Münzer, *Gnomon*, 1931, I, 34).

governing class was so small that its members were all linked together in a greater or less degree by ties of acquaintance or relationship. The influence of the family had always been a potent force at Rome, and important political questions were continually being affected by this factor. Naturally, these ties were always changing, and the political combinations in the Senate fluctuated with them.

Moreover, the strength of the personal factor in Roman politics must not be neglected. The political struggle of the period was not a combat of ideals but of individuals. Whether Caesar had any motive deeper than personal ambition is a moot point. It is certain that the other popular leaders were playing for their own hands alone. A politician depended for power on his own personal following rather than on a party, and each man changed his position as he thought fit. We may note that even when he was canvassing for the consulate Cicero did not know how individual nobles stood.[1]

It has been suggested that the 'nobiles' themselves formed a kind of political party; but in fact they were sharply divided on all the political questions of the day. Their only common aim was to restrict the higher offices of state as far as possible to themselves, that is, to the descendants of former consuls.[2] They formed an hereditary aristocracy which maintained its position as a governing class both by its control of the elections and by its undoubted capacity to rule. It is a striking fact that during these thirty years the consulate fell only four

[1] *ad Att.* I, 1, 2: *Cum perspexero voluntates nobilium, scribam ad te.*
[2] Gelzer, *op. cit.* p. 25: 'Die Nobilität fordert consularische Ahnen'. This definition is not universally accepted, but it seems most probable.

times to an outsider,[1] and only once, in 63, to a *novus homo* whose ancestors had held no curule office at all.[2] Inside the *nobilitas* was a still narrower circle comprising the four *gentes maiores* of the Patricians, which retained its social and political influence until the end of the Republic.[3]

Hence we may conclude with Strassburger that terms such as Optimates, Populares, Democrats, have in reality only a very limited application.[4] They were rather the catchwords of publicists and demagogues than the names of fixed parties. Even the 'extreme wing' of the nobility which Ciaceri postulates[5] was not a permanent association, but merely a temporary alliance which was continually changing. We must abandon all preconceived conceptions of party if we would understand the internal politics of the Roman Senate.

Yet, if there were no hard and fast parties in the Senate, every point at issue naturally revealed a difference of opinion; and it is interesting to trace through Cicero's speeches the various combinations which arose at different times. Cicero entered public life as the *protégé* of what we may call the 'moderate aristocracy', the spiritual successors of Scipio Aemilianus, and its members were probably behind him in his first two

[1] C. Scribonius Curio, 76; L. Gellius Poplicola, 72; L. Volcatius Tullus, 66; M. Tullius Cicero, 63. Cf. Cicero's boast that he had burst open the doors of privilege, *de leg. agr.* ii, 1, 3.

[2] The position of the *novus homo* is discussed by Schur (*op. cit.*) and by Joseph Vogt (*Homo Novus*, Stuttgart, 1926).

[3] Aemilii, Claudii, Cornelii, Fabii; v. Münzer, *op. cit.* 317.

[4] H. Strassburger, *Concordia Ordinum* (see bibliography).

[5] *Gnomon*, 1931, i, 34.

speeches. They had supported Sulla, but found themselves being squeezed out of office by the more extreme
oligarchs.[1] These moderates, whom Cicero styles *boni*,
have been well called the Whig Nobility of Rome.[2]
Prominent among them were the three brothers Aurelius Cotta, the eldest of whom, Gaius, largely restored
the powers of the tribunate during his consulate in 75.[3]
Their opponents were loosely labelled *pauci*: but this is
little more than an *ad hoc* term applied to those who dis-
agreed with Cicero on any particular issue, and it does
not denote a definite class. If Cicero referred it to the
extreme 'die-hards' in 70, he later used it to describe in
turn the supporters of the Rullan Law; Clodius and his
faction; and the Triumvirate.[4] One or two examples
will serve to show the fluctuations of Roman politics at
this time. Marcus Metellus supported Cicero in the *pro
Roscio*, but was attacked along with his brothers in the
speeches against Verres. On the other hand C. Curio,
who came under the heading of *pauci* in 70, has become
*bonus* by the time of the *Lex Manilia*; while Q. Catulus,
who supported Cicero in his attack on the law-courts in
70, was attacked four years later for his opposition to
the proposed command of Pompey. The Luculli also
helped Cicero against Verres; but their personal feelings
naturally led them to oppose him in the crisis of 66.
Hortensius, Cicero's great rival, was opposed to him

[1] Carcopino sees in the trial of Roscius the turning-point which marked
the downfall of Sulla; but it is unnecessary to regard Cicero's speech as
a manifesto of the nobility attacking the Sullan system *in toto*.

[2] Last, *C.A.H.* IX, 327.

[3] *Consul e media factione*; Sall. *Hist.* III, 48.

[4] *II in Verr.* I, 60, 155; *de leg. agr.* II, 25, 82; *pro Sest.* 31, 67; *ad fam.*
I, 8, 3.

throughout his early career, but even he was addressed as *bonus* in 61.[1]

## THE SCOPE OF THE SENATE

Greenidge epitomises the functions of the Senate as being 'to the people, probouleutic: to the magistrates, advisory'. The implication, that it had no plenary power of its own, was in theory correct; but in practice the Senate had become the supreme authority in the State, and more especially in the domain of foreign affairs.[2] This was a natural and inevitable development, for the Senate was far better qualified to deal with such questions than a vast and unwieldy assembly, ignorant of the point at issue, and easily swayed by the tongues of self-seeking tribunes. Moreover, the Republic had no Foreign Office, with a staff of permanent officials. It was essential to have some responsible committee for the handling of foreign policy; and the prestige acquired by the Senate in the Second Punic War had served to consolidate its authority still more firmly.

## THE SENATE AND THE ASSEMBLY

Even during the second century the Assembly had made some attempt to assert itself. For some time the Comitia refused to pass the formal declaration of war against Philip, and it attempted to resist the prolonga-

---

[1] *ad Att.* I, 14, 5. I am indebted to Strassburger for these examples.

[2] Cf. Polybius, VI, 13 fin.—ἐξ ὧν πάλιν ὁπότε τις ἐπιδημήσαι μὴ παρόντος ὑπάτου, τελείως ἀριστοκρατικὴ ἐφαίνεθ' ἡ πολιτεία. ὃ δὴ καὶ πολλοὶ τῶν Ἑλλήνων, ὁμοίως δὲ καὶ τῶν βασιλέων, πεπεισμένοι τυγχάνουσι, διὰ τὸ τὰ σφῶν πράγματα σχεδὸν πάντα τὴν σύγκλητον κυροῦν. The whole chapter furnishes an incisive summary of the powers of the Senate.

tion of Flamininus' command in Macedonia. But on the
whole the authority of the Senate was unimpugned, and,
as Rostovtzeff rightly says, it was not until the time of
the Gracchi that we find the doctrine definitely asserted
that the sovereignty of the People extended to foreign
affairs. In 133 Tiberius Gracchus proposed to handle
the bequest of Attalus of Pergamum in the Comitia
rather than in the Senate,[1] and his brother followed his
example by bringing his bill to regulate the taxation of
the new province directly before the People. In 107
Marius was given the command in Africa by a vote of
the Assembly, and it was by a similar means that Sulpicius transferred the Eastern command from Sulla to
Marius in 88. By Sulla's reforms, however, the supremacy of the Senate was once more established. He
definitely enacted that nothing could be laid before the
tribes without the previous sanction of the Senate; this
was a legal revival of what had been the law until 287,
and a sound custom until the time of the Gracchi. Still
more important was his degradation of the Tribunate, a
reform which muzzled the Assembly to some extent.
It was not until the full powers of the Tribunate had been
restored that the Assembly again began to question the
right of the Senate to conduct foreign affairs. In the
closing years of the Republic, however, we find it once
more interfering in such questions.

The Assembly played a great and increasing part in
the allotment of the special commands which figure so
largely in the history of the period. Here we may cite
one or two other instances of its new activity. In 67 the
tribunes Cornelius and Gabinius made a direct attack on

[1] Plutarch, *Ti. Gracchus*, 14.

the personal privileges of the senators by proposing to restrict the grant of 'legal dispensation' to the Assembly. Admittedly, the system by which a senator could obtain exemption from the action of any particular law was iniquitous, but this did not soften the opposition of the Senate. Eventually a compromise was reached, and the bill was passed in a modified form. 'Dispensations' were still to be passed by the Senate, but a fixed quorum of 200 members was instituted to prevent snap divisions. It was further conceded that if such a *privilegium* were subsequently brought before the Assembly, no tribune should be allowed to intervene with his veto. The material effect of this measure was less than the moral. From now on the Senate realised the power of the Assembly.

The year 59 saw a spate of comitial activity. Caesar's faithful henchman Vatinius confirmed Pompey's *acta*, and settled the question of the Asiatic contracts, by a *plebiscitum*. By the same method Caesar was granted Cisalpine Gaul as his province. But in this, as in all the crises of this decade, the Assembly was no more than the tool of the demagogues. It had no foreign policy of its own, and its interference in foreign affairs was usually confined to an arbitrary execution of the wishes of the Triumvirate. Its natural sympathies seem to have been with Caesar, and it was this fact that prompted Pompey's fear of his rival's return to Rome; but it was powerless against the great leaders, with their armies, and it remained a pawn in the game of high politics.

## THE SENATE AND THE MAGISTRATES

The consuls were usually amenable to the wishes of the
Senate. The growth of the Roman commonwealth had
naturally lessened the influence of the yearly magistrates,[1] while the governing class had perfected a
system of restricting election to high office to its
nominees. That *rara avis*, an 'opposition' consul, was
quickly awed by the accumulated prestige of the Senate,
as was shown by the subservience of Marius in 100.
Catulus, speaking as a good party man, used to say that
there had seldom been one *improbus* consul, and never
two together except in the year of Cinna's domination.[2]
It is true that L. Marcius Philippus, the consul for 91,
threatened that he would find his advisers elsewhere if
the Senate continued to support Drusus, but as a rule
the purely advisory nature of the Senate was forgotten.
Cicero can assert it as a platitude that 'all consuls obey
the Senate',[3] and it was left for Caesar to revive the
ancient independence of the office in 59. At first he
adopted a conciliatory attitude and introduced his land
bill into the Senate in the usual way, in person. But the
obstructive tactics of Cato led him to disregard con-
vention and turn directly to the Assembly; with the
same decision he broke through the attempts of the
Senate to fob him off with a worthless province. In
foreign policy too he pursued a line of his own. The
consuls were the traditional guardians of the kings who

---

[1] Cf. Gelzer, *N. Jahrb.* 1920, p. 15: 'In der späteren Republik war die
Stellung der Haüpter viel bedeutender als die jahrlich wechselnden
Magistrate'.

[2] *post red. ad sen.* 4, 9.          [3] *Ibid.* 7, 17.

were friends and allies of Rome,[1] and Caesar made this office a reality, much to his own profit. It is fairly certain that he granted Antiochus of Commagene recognition in return for a considerable sum,[2] and that he shared with Pompey the six thousand talents which Ptolemy Auletes paid—or promised to pay—for a senatorial resolution and a popular law by which he was re-established. Hence it is scarcely 'difficult to explain on what grounds of policy or business calculation Caesar supported the suit of his future antagonist, the German chieftain Ariovistus, who applied to the Senate for recognition as Amicus'.[3] Pliny tells us[4] that Ariovistus had sent some Indians in the previous year as a gift to Metellus Celer, the governor of Gaul, and it is only reasonable to suppose that Caesar received adequate, if less exotic, reward for his services.

As a rule, however, the Senate suffered rather from the interference of the tribunes than of the consuls. We have seen how Gabinius and Cornelius allied themselves with the Assembly to attack the privileges of the Senate. The tribunes furnished too a useful tool by which the military leaders could acquire their commands. Still worse was it when the tribunes began playing for their own hands. The years 59 and 58 furnish the most notorious examples of tribunicial activity. Vatinius profited from the example of his illustrious master, and 'rose from poverty to wealth in a single year through

[1] *pro Sest.* 30, 64: *In eius magistratus tutela reges atque exterae nationes semper fuerunt.* Cf. also Caesar, *bell. civ.* III, 107: *controversias regum ad populum Romanum et ad se, quod esset consul, pertinere existimans.*

[2] *ad Q.F.* II, 12, 2: *Togam praetextam, quam erat adeptus Caesare consule.*

[3] Cary, *C.A.H.* IX, 518.      [4] Pliny, *N.H.* II, 67, 170.

trafficking with kings'.[1] Clodius, tribune in 58, is the target of repeated attacks by Cicero. The orator's sweeping generalisations are based on the two known cases of Deiotarus and his son-in-law Brogitarus, the chieftain of the Trocmi, to whom he granted the royal title in return for a consideration. Nor was his generosity confined to words, for he also bestowed part of his father-in-law's kingdom on his new *protégé*.

To Clodius too was due the confiscation of Cyprus. He had a personal grudge against the reigning Ptolemy,[2] while such an expedition provided an excellent means of securing the honourable banishment of the insufferable Cato.

The blatant corruption of Vatinius and Clodius was pernicious, but its effects must not be exaggerated. Most of the tribunes had neither the ability nor the ambition to interfere in the conduct of foreign affairs. When Curio, as tribune in 50, made an abortive proposal to annex Numidia, he was acting merely as the mouthpiece of the absent Caesar. The lesser magistrates played a still less important part. Cicero makes an obscure reference[3] to the activities of a certain Staienus in his quaestorship (77 B.C.), who had apparently set up statues inscribed '*Reges ab se in gratiam esse reductos*'; but in the absence of further evidence we can attach little importance to this.[4]

---

[1] *in Vat.* 12, 29.

[2] Appian, *bell. civ.* II, 23, 85.

[3] *pro Cluentio*, 36, 101. The reference is perhaps to Mithridates. Cicero also terms Staienus *nummarius interpres pacis et concordiae* (*ib.*).

[4] I owe much of the material in this section to R. O. Jolliffe (*Phases of Corruption in Roman Administration*).

## THE POWERS OF THE SENATE

In foreign affairs particularly the Senate had acquired wide plenipotentiary powers. It was the permanent Foreign Office of Rome, and it had always conducted preliminary negotiations with foreign states. Cicero refers to it in laudatory terms as the 'haven and refuge of kings, peoples, nations'.[1] After the surrender of Albinus in Africa in 110 it had re-enunciated the principle that no valid treaty could be made without its own consent and that of the Roman People. This finally determined the old controversy, whether the general in the field had the right to make binding treaties or only an armistice for a year (*indutiae*) while the Senate deliberated;[2] but there still remained the possibility of the dormant claims of the People being revived. In 78 this question was called into the open. The Gaditani applied to the Senate for the renewal of a treaty made with a subordinate general during the Punic Wars. The Senate, under the leadership of the consuls Catulus and Lepidus, either renewed the treaty or made a fresh one without consulting the People. Twenty-two years later Cicero discusses the matter at length in the speech For Balbus. He does not impugn the validity of the treaty as a working agreement but he categorically denies that it can be regarded as sacrosanct.[3] This sophistical solution maintained the theoretical supremacy of the People,

[1] *de officiis*, ii, 8, 26.

[2] Cf. Livy, ix, 8; Plutarch, *Tib. Gracchus*, 7; *de offic.* iii, 30, 109; Sallust, *Jugurtha*, 39.

[3] Cf. *pro. Balb.* 15, 34: *Nec vero haec oratio mea ad infirmandum foedus Gaditanorum pertinet* and *ib.* 35: *Sacrosanctum enim nihil potest esse, nisi quod per populum plebemve sancitum est.*

but in practice even when a treaty actually was presented to the Comitia for confirmation this must have been a mere form. Except in rare cases the Senate was the sole arbiter of war and peace. It was by now established that all treaties made in the field had to be ratified by the Senate. Sulla himself had to obtain the confirmation of the Senate for the so-called Peace of Dardanus. And that this confirmation was no empty formality is shown by the Senate's very proper refusal to confirm Pompey's arrangements in the East *en bloc*. Caesar overrode many of the powers of the Senate; but although he made his own decisions in Syria, even he refused to grant the Jews any permanent privileges without a decree of the Senate.

The routine business of foreign administration was still more completely in the hands of the Senate. To it belonged the adjudication of the claims of the free cities, and it could revoke their 'charters' at its pleasure.[1] For instance, it is expressly laid down in the fifth clause of the *Lex de Termessibus* of 70 that the Senate shall have the right to override the clause forbidding the billeting of troops in the town. Similarly the Senate was the body to which the client and allied princes turned themselves, except when a magistrate interested himself in their affairs for his own ends. The part it played in the appointment of a provincial governor, and the control it exercised over his administration, will be discussed later.

## THE SENATE AND THE EQUITES

One of the most important considerations affecting the policy of the Senate was the relation that existed between it and the Equites. From the constitutional point

[1] See Hardy, *Roman Laws and Charters*, p. 95.

of view the Equites had no privileges apart from a share in the jury-courts, but they formed such an influential part of the body-politic that the Senate could never afford to neglect their opinion.

The Senate and the Equites were, as Heitland says, 'natural allies torn asunder by C. Gracchus',[1] and the democratic leader certainly did his best to establish them as a permanent opposition. Sulla weakened them by taking away from them the control of the law-courts, by thinning their ranks in the proscriptions, and by promoting three hundred of them to the Senate. The orthodox view is that from this time on the Equites regarded the Senate with bitter hatred, but there is much to be said for Schur's opinion[2] that Sulla's reforms really brought the rivalry between Senate and Equites to an end. The extension of the franchise had meant a large influx into the Equestrian ranks of landed and conservative Italians. The increased number of offices provided more openings for ambitious Equestrians, and there was nothing to prevent an Eques embarking on a public career and gaining entry to the Senate. Cicero was not the only Eques of note who secured a seat in the 'Upper House'. The interests of the orders were sufficiently coincident for them to work on the whole in harmony. The *Lex Aurelia*, by which the Equites received a fair share in the administration of justice, threw them into closer contact with the Senate, and removed their main grievance. Already in the Verrine Orations we see a foreshadowing of that *concordia ordinum* which was

[1] Cf. Varro, *de vita pop. Rom.* lib. IV: *C. Gracchus equestri ordini iudicia tradidit ac bicipitem civitatem fecit*.

[2] W. Schur, 'Homo Novus', *Bonn. Jahrb.* 1929, p. 54.

Cicero's ideal; while speaking as a senator to senators, he pays marked attention to the Equites and deliberately appeals for their support.

Throughout the following decade the Equites drew nearer and nearer to the Senate. If, as Greenidge suggests, their provincial interests led them to oppose the Senate, their fear of revolution at home attached them to it, and this was a much more potent force. They joined with the Senate to oppose the tribunes Cornelius and Gabinius in 67, while in the same year the *Lex Roscia*[1] which gave them a social standing was a deliberate attempt on the part of the Senate to cement their allegiance. Cicero suggests that this measure was due to an urgent popular demand, but Stein has refuted this statement.[2] The promotion of the Equites was directed rather against the unprivileged masses than against the Senate. This is proved by the subsequent unpopularity of Otho among the people, a fact which is mentioned by both Plutarch and Pliny.[3] It is true that the Equites supported the *Lex Manilia*, but so did many of the Senators; and during the next four years the concord of the orders grew steadily stronger. Fear of Catiline accentuated the natural conservatism of the Equites. The prospect of new fields to conquer put them in a good humour, while the growing power of Pompey inclined them to support the Senate as a counterweight; for the Equites, although always willing to use Pompey's services, had no more desire than the Senate for a military tyranny. Moreover, the

[1] By this law too the Equestrian census was first definitely fixed.

[2] Cic. *pro Corn. ap. Asc.* 107; A. Stein, *Der römische Ritterstand.* He suggests that the *Lex Roscia* replaced a former law repealed by Sulla, but this is improbable.

[3] Plut. *Cic.* 13; Pliny, *n.h.* VII, 117.

old economic distinctions were breaking down. The strict regulations which forbade a Senator to engage in trade were falling into disuse,[1] and new social and family connections tended to obliterate the distinction between the orders. The year 63 shows the high-water mark of the new harmony. Cicero often recalls the enthusiastic support he received from the Equites during the decisive sittings of the Senate. But this harmony was based mainly on the selfish interests of the Equites, who were nervous for their capital, and Cicero was mistaken when he interpreted it as a spontaneous demonstration of loyalty and goodwill. The Equites were rarely actuated by altruistic motives, and Cicero himself was bound to confess later that he had only 'glued up' the alliance.[2]

The complete suppression of Catiline removed the chief bond between the Senate and the Equites. Their actual estrangement was due to two incidents. The first was the attempt of the Senate to make the Equites liable for charges of corruption. Cato's proposal to bring the law into line with the new judicial arrangements was as inopportune as it was just. Hence it was opposed by Cicero, who was willing to sacrifice principle to practical considerations. The details are obscure, but the proceedings apparently drew themselves out, as the question was brought up in November of 61, was still unsettled in January of 60, and is mentioned again in June of the same year.[3] Even if Cicero's attempt to burke the bill

[1] *II in Verr.* v, 18, 45: *antiquae sunt istae leges et mortuae.*

[2] *ad Att.* i, 17, 10: *illam a me conglutinatam concordiam.* Too much importance must not, however, be attached to the use of the word *conglutino.*

[3] *ad Att.* i, 17, 8; i, 18, 3; ii, 8.

was successful, the affair could scarcely be expected to improve the relations between the orders.

More important was the question of the Asiatic contracts. We have two accounts of this, from Cicero and from a scholiast.[1] Of these the former is the more reliable; for Cicero was an eye-witness, and despite his close connection with the tax-farmers his account is much less favourable to them. The scholiast attributes the tax-farmers' losses to barbarian invasions of the province. Cicero says that they had bid too high in their greed, and this is confirmed by Suetonius.[2] The request was probably introduced in the Senate by the leaders of the tax-farmers in person,[3] and it was supported by the 'popular' leaders for their own ends. That Cicero too should endorse the proposal is surprising in view of his frank condemnation of the whole business. He was impelled not only by a strong sense of gratitude for the support given him by the Equites in 63, but also by motives of expediency, for he did not wish to throw them into the arms of Caesar and Crassus. 'What is more impudent', he wrote to Atticus,[4] 'than the broken contracts of the tax-farmers? Yet the financial sacrifice must be made, to hold the order.' The proposal met with the strong opposition of Metellus Celer, the consul designate, and of Cato, who guided his political life by principle alone.[5] His policy of obstruction was successful, but it is worth noting that the Senate never went so

[1] *ad Att.* I, 17, 9; Schol. *Bob. Hild.* 133. v. Strassburger, *op. cit.*

[2] Suetonius, *Julius Caesar*, 20.

[3] Among them seems to have been the elder Plancius (*pro Plancio*, 14, 35).

[4] *ad Att.* II, 1, 8.

[5] Cf. *de officiis*, III, 22, 88: *omnia publicanis negare, multa sociis.*

far as to give the Equites a definite refusal. The whole
episode shows both the Equites' complete disregard of
the *concordia ordinum*, and their growing influence in
the State. There has rarely been a more arrant attempt
on the part of one faction of the community to intimidate
the national government in its own interests.

The matter was finally settled by Caesar as consul on
very generous terms. It is possible that he received a
loan from the Equites in return; at all events they were
now firmly attached to him.[1] It is true that in 59 there
was a hostile demonstration made against Caesar and
Pompey in the theatre, to which they replied by a threat
to repeal the *Lex Roscia*, but Cicero made too much of
this. The demonstrators were not necessarily the leading
tax-farmers, but probably only the younger and more
irresponsible members of the Equites, while in any case
it was a merely temporary ebullition of feeling. The
Equites knew where their interests lay, and guided their
actions accordingly. Their attitude towards Cicero's
banishment is instructive. Despite his hopes they raised
no protest. It is true they helped in his recall, but this
had little significance, and even he began to despair of
his ideal. Moreover, in spite of his claim to have broken
the barriers of the nobility, there seems to have been a
recrudescence of the old spirit of rivalry between the
orders. Laterensis, a noble, complained that an 'Eques'
was preferred to him; Caelius, an Eques, regarded it as
a misfortune to have a noble rival.[2] This ill-feeling was
accentuated by the vexed question of the extension of
the penal restrictions mentioned above; perhaps we may

---

[1] Cf. Meyer, *Caesars Monarchie*, p. 75.
[2] *pro Planc.* 7, 17; *ad fam.* VIII, 2, 2; cf. *pro Cael.* 2, 4.

see in the attacks on Rabirius Postumus, Cluentius and Oppius an attempt on the part of the Senate to extend the application of the bribery laws. In each case Cicero appeals to the non-senatorial majority of the court not to establish a predecent dangerous to itself by condemning the accused.[1]

Cicero still made desperate efforts to retain the good-will of the Equites, both by his continual letters of re-commendation and by his own subservience to the *publicani*, who formed, as he said, 'the bloom of the equestrian order'; but it was impossible to re-establish the concord of the orders. It is true that during the civil war most of the Equites threw in their lot with Pompey and the Senate,[2] but they were perhaps impelled by fear lest, if Caesar won, he might inaugurate a massacre of the moneyed classes after the prescription of Sulla. The Equites who fell at Pharsalus sacrificed themselves not for the Republic but for the sacred cause of property.

It remains to consider the part played by the Equites as a body in determining the policy, and especially the foreign policy, of the Senate. The Equites only became a force to be reckoned with after the reforms of C. Grac-chus; it has been estimated that in 150 the amount of Roman capital engaged in equestrian contracts was not more than 2 per cent.[3] But after 123 the grant of new contracts combined with the control of the jury-courts

[1] But Cicero may be deliberately exaggerating this point. It seems that many even of the Senate had no desire to extend these laws, for when Pompey made a proposal to this effect in 55 B.C., the Senate joined with the Equites to oppose it (*pro Rab. Post.* 6, 13).

[2] Some of them, however, remained faithful to Caesar: cf. Caelius, *ap. ad fam.* VIII, 18, 2.

[3] Tenney Frank, *An Economic Survey of Ancient Rome*, I, p. 157.

to give them great if indirect political influence. Stein denies that the *publicani* can be identified with the Equites, but they were certainly drawn from their ranks, and it was the Equites who consistently represented their interests.[1] Their power was seen in 120; Phrygia had been given by Aquilius to the king of Pontus, but the grant was revoked and the district was declared 'free', to be exploited by Roman capitalists. Perhaps the grant had never been confirmed by Rome, but there was more than a suspicion of double-dealing about the whole business. In 118 the Equites gave strong support to the founding of a new citizen colony at Narbo Martius. They were instrumental in forcing through the *Lex Mamilia* which appointed a commission to investigate charges of treachery in 110–109, while three years later it was an alliance of Equites and People that elected Marius to the consulate.

Whatever their motive, the Equites were right in pressing for firm measures against Jugurtha. In 92 came a flagrant abuse of their power, when Rutilius Rufus was condemned for extortion as a direct result of his upright behaviour as a legate in Asia. This case has been emphasised because it provided an excellent handle for senatorial historians, and also because Cicero regarded Rutilius as his great model.

It was the opposition of the Equites that caused the failure of Livius Drusus. His proposal to promote three hundred Equites to the Senate did not compensate for his judicial reforms and his attempt to make the Equites liable for charges of corruption, while he roused them

[1] Cf. Dio Cassius, XXXVIII, 7: πᾶσαί τε γὰρ αἱ τελωνίαι δι' αὐτῶν τῶν ἱππέων ἐγίγνοντο.

still further when he began to debase the currency. In 89 the tribunes Papirius and Plautius attacked the monopoly of the Equites in the law-courts and reduced the weight of the *as*; but when the praetor Asellio attempted to protect debtors by reviving the old laws against usury he was murdered at the instigation of the Equites.

For the first decade after the Sullan restoration the Equites played little part in high politics, but they again came into prominence during the Mithridatic War. It was perhaps their influence that caused the bequest of Bithynia to be accepted. They were certainly responsible for the recall of Lucullus, and we shall see later the significance of this step. Equestrian interests appear again in Crassus' proposal to subject Egypt to tribute in 65,[1] while Pompey's settlement of the East was largely governed by consideration for the order. The question of the tax-farming of Asia is obscure, but Pompey probably confirmed, if he did not re-establish, the tax-farming system in the province.[2] In Syria, and probably too in Judaea and Cilicia, he combined both systems by organising local taxation districts, which were farmed out separately.[3] The agrarian proposals of Rullus were a counter-attempt to bid for Equestrian support, for by them employment was to be found for two hundred Equites as surveyors.

The story of Piso and Gabinius is illuminating. As

[1] This seems to be a reasonable assumption from *de leg. ag.* ii, 17, 44.

[2] Rice Holmes concludes that Sulla had left the tax-farming of Asia untouched.

[3] In any case, we can infer from *de prov. cons.* 5, 10 that the Roman Equites were given a considerable share in the profits of his eastern conquests.

consuls in 58 they had been actively hostile to the
Equites; perhaps Gabinius was influenced by his sympathy with the Catilinarian cause which the Equites had
opposed even more vigorously than the Senate. He
resisted the tentative efforts of the Equites to recall
Cicero, and he sent L. Aelius Lamia, a rich Eques, into
exile on this account. He threatened the order generally
with death and proscription, while in the provinces both
these magistrates used their position to vent their spleen
upon the Equites. Piso in Macedonia delivered up a
Roman Eques to his debtors in return for a bribe, while
Cicero asserts that Gabinius did the same in Syria. They
were both prosecuted on their return, largely through
the hostile influence of the Equites. Cicero must have
found the defence of Gabinius one of the bitterest pills
he had to swallow at the behest of the Triumvirs.[1]
Pompey and Crassus, although they felt bound to defend
their tool Gabinius, thought it worth their while to
cultivate the Equites, as is shown by the conference they
held with members of that order in 55.[2]

The influence of the *publicani* was still more apparent
in the provinces. In Sicily, Asia and later Syria, the
tribute was directly farmed out to Roman capitalists.
They were responsible for the collection of customs-
duties and pasture-rents throughout the Empire, and
they contracted for the collection of arrears of taxation
which might otherwise have had to be written off as bad
debts. The revenue from all the public lands passed

[1] Piso and Gabinius: see *post. red. in sen.* 5, 12; 12, 32; *de dom.* 21,
55; *pro Sest.* 12, 29; *ad fam.* xii, 29; *in Pis.* 35, 86; *de prov. cons.* 5, 10;
Dio, xxxix, 59, 2; *in Pis.* 20, 45; *ad. Q.F.* iii, 2, 2.

[2] *ad Att.* iv, 11, 1.

through their hands. They managed the vast estates of the former kinds of Bithynia and the old crown lands of Macedonia.

The *publicani* owed their power in the provinces to the vested interests standing behind them at Rome. Each company was composed of a vast number of share-holders,[1] and we see from Cicero's letters how important it was that the governor should not risk incurring their displeasure.[2] He urges Quintus to keep on good terms with them, and begs him to remember 'their high position, and how much we owe to that order'. He often writes to governors on behalf of individuals or companies, and he even asks a propraetor of Bithynia to allow one of these gentry to fix his own price for the pasture-rents. Lentulus Spinther, the consul for 57, apparently dared to protect the provincials against the tax-farmers. Cicero's letter to him needs no comment: 'Just after I had written you, I received your letter about the tax-farmers. I cannot disapprove of your fairness towards them; but I wish you could have had the good luck to avoid striking against the acts or intentions of that order which you have always honoured. Of course I shall not cease to defend your decrees. But you know what men are, and you remember what bitter enemies these fellows were to Scaevola. My advice is this; if it is at all possible, either reconcile that order to yourself or propitiate it in some way. I know it is not easy, but I think it is within your power.' On the other hand he praised Murena for the help he had given the Equites in

[1] Polybius, VI, 17, 3.

[2] *ad Q.F.* I, 1, 35; *ad fam.* XIII, 65, 1; *ad fam.* I, 9, 26; *pro Murena*, 20, 42.

recovering their bad debts while he was governor of Gaul. When he himself took a province he found it extremely difficult to satisfy both the provincials and the tax-farmers. He was continually wavering between his high ideals of government and his desire not to offend the equestrian interests behind the *publicani*; but if a conflict of interests could not be avoided it was usually the provincials who suffered. He was himself an Eques by birth, and his own sympathies combined with his ideal of the harmony of the orders to deter him from opposing the powerful capitalist class of Rome.

## THE PERSONNEL OF THE SENATE

Cineas, the ambassador of Pyrrhus, had styled the Senate an assembly of kings; and it is true that its personnel was extremely well adapted for the business of government. Its members were bred to rule from their youth up, while, as Greenidge puts it, 'the race for honours provided stimuli sufficient to keep a counsellor of Rome up to a high standard of efficiency'. Through the maintenance of the elective system the Senate was primarily based on the People; the regularity with which office fell to members of the nobility was partly due to the force of corruption, but the personal prestige of the governing class must have had some weight. Moreover, it is a fallacy to suppose that a corrupt method of election necessarily produces a bad governing body. Many of the most famous English statesmen of the eighteenth century were returned through the medium of the pocket borough. Gelzer states[1] that the political aristocracy

[1] *Op. cit.* p. 70.

took the lead in oratory and jurisprudence. The average Roman senator was imbued with the spirit of public service. The history of the Roman nobility is not an 'unmixed tale of degeneration' but 'a story of achievement and sacrifice'.[1]

The average senator was content to serve his country without clamouring for extraordinary commands. It is true that he desired high office, but to gain the consulate he had first to undergo a long term of routine work in minor offices at home and abroad. When his command terminated he was willing to retire into private life without the petulant regrets of a Pompey or a Crassus. We may instance the way in which Metellus Pius punctiliously discharged his army in 71 after crossing the Alps on his return from Spain. Such strict adhesion to the constitution was the rule rather than the exception. In 59 C. Vergilius, governor of Sicily, although he was on intimate terms with Cicero, would not allow him to enter his province because it was within the proscribed distance from Italy, nor does Cicero blame him for his refusal.[2]

Even the senators who have been pilloried by history were not without their merits. M. Porcius Cato has been immortalised as the unpractical pedant whose unctuous righteousness became a fetish. In actual fact he was an upright if not brilliant senator with considerable business ability; he has suffered from the misrepresentation which always attaches itself to the man who

[1] Münzer, *op. cit.* p. 329; cf. Aelius, *ap. ad fam.* VIII, 5, 1: *Omnia desiderantur ab eo...qui publico negotio praepositus est.*

[2] Clodius had introduced a bill by which Cicero was forbidden to stay within five hundred miles of Italy. See *pro Planc.* 40, 95, and cf. *ad fam.* II, 19, 2: *familiarissimus noster.*

knows what his policy is and sticks to it. He believed in the supremacy of the Senate *per se*. Hence he could not sympathise with Cicero's efforts to conciliate the Equites; and he was frequently criticised by the orator for his Utopian views. But at heart Cicero admired him as much as did most of his contemporaries. He had had much military experience against Spartacus and in Macedonia, and he was widely travelled. There is no reason to doubt the financial integrity of his organisation of Cyprus. He carried his opposition to the Triumvirs to extreme lengths because he was far-sighted enough to see what a danger they constituted to the State. That he knew when to yield is shown by his advice to Cicero to capitulate to Clodius. Gelzer's praise of him is warm but not excessive[1]. The reception accorded to him on his return from the East is proof of his popularity with all classes. He may have been obstinate, but the regard in which he was held by his friends is instanced by M. Petreius' fiery reply to Caesar in 59—'I will rather sit in prison with Cato than with you in the Senate'.[2]

Similarly, our respect for Bibulus increases when we read of his fortitude in carrying on after his two sons had been slain in a mutiny of Gabinius' soldiers in Egypt. Partisan accounts of his consulship have led us to regard him as a man impervious to reason, who adopted a petulant dog-in-the-manger attitude when he could not get his own way. In reality he was a man with definite principles, and he stuck to them in the face of

[1] *N. Jahrb.* XLV, 27: 'Der Name des jüngeren Cato enthält in der Tat alles was zugunsten der römischen Gesellschaft zur Zeit Ciceros gesagt werden kann.' Cf. *ad Att.* II, 1, 8; II, 5, 1; also Meyer, *Caesars Monarchie*, p. 220.

[2] Dio Cassius, XXXVIII, 3, 2.

formidable opposition. He certainly came out of the disgraceful scenes of 59 with more dignity than his colleague, whatever we may think of Caesar's reforms. His generalship, too, has been unjustly belittled through Cicero's sneers; the governor of Cilicia was, in fact, jealous of his neighbour's triumph.

The consular *fasti* of the period contain some sixty names, of which the overwhelming majority belong to the 'noble' families. Some of these are of little political significance and must be considered happy in that they have no history; but in many cases we can trace the outlines of a career, and even establish some sort of a personality behind it. It is impossible to deal with each one in detail; but as we read through the lists we are struck with the way in which solid administrative talent seems to run in families.[1] Admittedly, bribery played a large part in the elections, but it was not by itself sufficient to carry a man to the highest office in the State. The three brothers Aurelius Cotta held the consulate within a decade. Lucullus himself was directly succeeded in office by his brother Marcus. By adopting Q. Metellus Pius as his colleague in 80, Sulla had definitely allied himself with the noble families. No fewer than six members of this family attained the consulate in these thirty years,[2] while cadets of the family filled many of the lower offices. The family names of Lentulus and Spinther also recur; a Marcellus was consul in the two successive years 51 and 50.

---

[1] It is interesting to recall that one of Queen Victoria's Cabinets was known as the Hotel Cecil, from the number of members of that house it contained.

[2] '*Fato Metelli....*'; see table at end of chapter.

A word must be said of the recognised leaders of the
Senate. P. Servilius Vatia Isauricus was consul in 79,
and survived to become the Grand Old Man of the
Senate. His consulate was chiefly noteworthy for his
attempt to prevent Pompey's unconstitutional triumph.
For the five following years he held a special command
against the pirates in Cilicia, and he seems to have met
with considerable success both in pacifying the coast
and in his punitive expeditions into the hinterland. In
74 he celebrated a triumph. He was a juror in the trial
of Verres, and was addressed by Cicero as *bonus*. He
supported the *Lex Manilia*, probably through his personal feud with the Luculli; he was one of the *consulares*
who urged strong measures against Catiline; and he was
active in promoting Cicero's recall in 57. When the
restoration of Ptolemy Auletes was proposed in 56, he
succeeded in adjourning the matter *sine die*; the same
year he attacked Gabinius and Piso for their misgovernment in the provinces. He was elected censor in 54, and
lived in honoured retirement until his death ten years
later; throughout his life he commanded the respect both
of his peers and of the people.[1]

Q. Lutatius Catulus was another outstanding figure in
the Senate. As consul in 78 he had to devote most of
his time to combating the intrigues of his colleague
Lepidus; but besides instigating the *Lex Plotia de vi*, he
showed his interest in foreign affairs by renewing the
treaty with Gades,[2] and by procuring a vote of thanks
for the foreign shipmasters, Asclepiades, Polystratus
and Meniscus, for their services in the Italian war.[3] He

---

[1] Schol. *Gronov.* 442: *florebat, in senatu princeps erat, amabatur a populo.*
[2] *pro Cael.* 29, 70; *pro Balb.* 15, 34.        [3] *C.I.L.* 1, 2, 588.

was a conservative who saw the faults of the Senate; and as a judge in the Verres case he was praised by Cicero for his condemnation of judicial corruption. He opposed the Gabinian and Manilian Laws with his brother-in-law Hortensius, but his arguments were heard with respect by the people. His censorship with Crassus led to a position of stalemate; while his feud with Caesar was increased by his defeat in the pontifical election. He was the first to oppose Caesar's mild motion in the debate on the Catilinarian conspirators, and he was hailed by Cicero as a champion of the Optimate policy. His high character, his sincerity, and his patriotism were recognised by his contemporaries no less than his prudence in counsel and his steadfastness in action.[1]

Of L. Licinius Lucullus we shall speak later at greater length. His brother Marcus (consul 73) also took a prominent part in public life. As praetor in 75 he had condemned C. Antonius for extortion in Greece. During his consulate he settled the quarrel between Oropus and the tax-farmers. As governor of Macedonia he fully earned his triumph by his exploits against the Thracians and Moesians. His instinct for good government led him to support Cicero against Verres; he also threw his weight on the side of law and order during the Catilinarian conspiracy. Like many nobles of the day, he indulged his aesthetic tastes; but we have Varro's word for it that he never allowed his interest in his fish-ponds to affect his public life.[2]

Q. Hortensius (consul 69), a staunch upholder of the

---

[1] See especially *de imp. Cn. Pomp.* 17, 51; *pro Sest.* 47, 101; *de offic.* I, 22, 76; Plut. *Crass.* 6, 13; Dio, xxxvII, 46; *ad Att.* I, 20, 3.

[2] Varro, *r.r.* III, 3, 10; 17, 8.

Senate's supremacy, was throughout his life the great rival of Cicero. It was he who attacked Quinctius. He defended Verres and opposed the Gabinian and Manilian Laws. He was closely connected with the Luculli and other noble families, and was the leader of the more florid style of Roman oratory. In his consistent opposition to the broad views of Cicero he perhaps provides the nearest approach to a party politician, in our sense, in ancient Rome. He is to be found acting with him only after he had thrown in his lot with the Senate. His influence is shown by the order of speaking in the Senate in 61, where he ranked fourth, after Piso, Cicero and Catulus. He was not interested in foreign administration and did not take a province after his praetorship. In 68, despite the prospects of war between Crete and Rome, he refused Macedonia and Achaia, with the conduct of the war, in favour of his colleague, Metellus Creticus.

C. Calpurnius Piso (consul 67) was an ardent supporter of the Sullan constitution. He stoutly opposed the legislation of Cornelius and Gabinius; but his own stringent bribery law shows that he was no mere reactionary. As governor of Narbonensis he reduced the Allobroges. Accused by Caesar of extortion on his return, he was defended by Cicero and acquitted. He supported Cicero against Catiline, but his own pre-eminence in the Senate led to a marked coolness between them. In 59, the year before his death, he tried in vain to mediate between Caesar and Bibulus.

But by the closing decade of the period these leaders were either dead or retired from active public life, and successors were strangely hard to find. The intrigues

of the Triumvirs had thrown Rome into a state of confusion; and the future was so uncertain that there was
little temptation for the Roman noble to enter public
life. Some retired to their estates and amused themselves
with more or less innocent pleasures; some followed
Cato and his policy of intransigeance; the better sort
occupied themselves with administrative duties in the
provinces. Such was P. Lentulus Spinther, the consul
for 57. He was a consistent supporter of Cicero and was
largely responsible for his recall. It was suggested that
he should be entrusted with the restoration of Ptolemy,
but the proposal fell through. He proceeded quietly to
Cilicia after his year of office, and there showed himself
a wise and liberal governor.

From such material, however, Cicero could not hope
to build up a counter-force to Caesar, and hence the
Senate was forced to accept the dangerous alliance of
Pompey. When it came to open war, most of the nobles,
Cicero and Lentulus among them, followed Pompey
from motives of class and personal loyalty, or because
they regarded him, despite his faults, as the champion
of the Republic. A few, from far-sighted patriotism or
for personal advantage, faced the issue more frankly.
In P. Servilius Isauricus the younger we have a good
representative of this transition period between republic
and empire. He inherited traditions of service from his
father. In 61 he supported Cato against the tax-farmers;
five years later he opposed Pompey on the Egyptian
question. As praetor with Cato in 54 he showed his
regard for the constitution by attempting to hinder the
delayed triumph of Pomptinus over the Allobroges. In
49, realising that the Rump under Pompey could no

longer be regarded as the Senate,[1] he was one of the first senators to join Caesar. He did good service as consul in 48. From 46 to 44 he was proconsul of Asia. Cicero praised him as an excellent governor and numerous inscriptions in his honour have been found.[2] He was not the only governor of the period who settled down to his task in the provinces without worrying about the wider politics of the day.

## APPENDIX

### *The family table of the Metelli, adapted from Pauly-Wissowa*

Dates of the consulate are given in parentheses

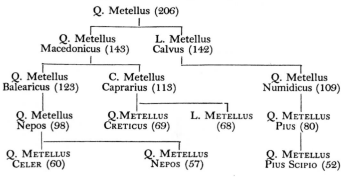

---

[1] It is true that a numerical majority of the Senate followed Pompey to the East. But the flight from Rome must have caused such a loss of prestige that the historical analogy will stand.

[2] Inscriptions collected in Pauly-Wissowa, ii, 2 A, 1800.

## CHAPTER II

# THE FOREIGN POLICY OF
# THE SENATE

## THE ROMAN ATTITUDE TOWARDS
## FOREIGN AFFAIRS

'F ROM 133 B.C. a consistent foreign policy was impossible; it is against a background of civil contention that the action of foreign politics must now be viewed.'[1] It is true that the tribunate of T. Gracchus inaugurated a period in which the domestic history of the city was of preponderating importance, yet problems of external policy could not be entirely neglected.

Rome in general, and the Senate in particular, is often charged with a lack of interest in foreign affairs. There is some justification for this reproach. After Cicero's return from Sicily in 74 he was mortified by the apathy shown to his achievements. Perhaps he had exaggerated the importance of his charge; but a similar experience befell Pompey in spite of his far greater exploits. When he addressed the People for the first time after his return from the East he was asked his opinion on a point of law; he turned to the Senate, and the consul Messala tried to draw him by raising a constitutional problem.[2] It

---

[1] Tenney Frank.

[2] *pro Planc.* 26, 64–5; *ad Att.* I, 14; but we cannot build too much on these three instances. One of the most eminent Viceroys of India, Lord Irwin, was in recent years welcomed home with less ceremony and interest than a third-rate film actor.

must be said in fairness that his work overseas was not
deliberately slighted: it was merely that all parties at
Rome thought it of primary importance to discover what
political attitude he would take up. In fact, throughout
the period the critical nature of domestic politics tended
to obscure the broader issues.[1] At such a time senators
did not care to absent themselves from Rome, and provincial commands became increasingly unpopular.
Caelius states that the consuls of 51 were doing their
best to evade the onus of office, while Cicero regarded
his term in Cilicia as a year in exile.[2]

But this lack of interest must not be exaggerated.
Cicero's nostalgia was exceptional, and was one of those
strangely Gallic traits of his which Boissier has pointed
out. He himself admits that his reluctance to take a
province was still unusual. Moreover, his own interest
in the right administration of the provinces is shown by
the fact that one of the chief charges he brings against
the Senate in 50 is its neglect to arrange for the provincial government. Yet he does concentrate on domestic politics in his writings, and it is only from stray
hints that we gather the continued interest of the Senate
in foreign affairs. Murena, returning from his province
of Gaul in 63, was received by a vast crowd which included 'many of the most respectable members of the
Senate'.[3] Nor was this interest confined to words, as
the Senate was continually granting help to governors
in time of need. We may instance the extraordinary

---

[1] *pro Planc.* 26, 63: *Ita multa Romae geruntur ut vix ea quae fiunt in provinciis audiantur.*

[2] Cf. *ad fam.* viii, 10, 3; *ad Att.* v, 15, 1.

[3] *ad Att.* v, 2, 3; vii, 7, 5; *pro Murena*, 33, 69.

grant of eighteen million denarii to Lucullus for the construction of a fleet in 74.

The Senate always showed a particular interest in the affairs of Gaul, because of its proximity. In 60, rumours of the Helvetic migration caused great alarm at Rome, and the Senate took vigorous action which may best be described in Cicero's own words: 'Just now the affairs of Gaul have been most disturbing. Our good friends the Aedui have been defeated in battle; there is no doubt that the Helvetii are in arms and are making inroads into the province. The Senate has decreed that the consuls shall cast lots for the two Gauls. Levies are to be held and all leave is stopped. Ambassadors are being sent with full powers to visit the states of Gaul and prevent them joining the Helvetii.'[1] Caesar's victories relieved this fear; and the Senate expressed its gratitude to him by thrice decreeing a *supplicatio* in his honour. Is it too guileless to accept these as voluntary and sincere tributes to one whom the Senate was bound to regard, politically, as its enemy?

The unpopularity of Piso and Gabinius on their return in 54 was increased by the disgrace they had brought upon the Roman arms.[2] Even in the stress of the year 51 the Senate found time to renew an old treaty with the Rhodians.[3] The same year news of a fresh movement by the Parthians caused great excitement at Rome, and the question of what was to be done temporarily eclipsed the domestic problems of the day.

The numerous laws against extortion and misgovernment, while providing an illuminating commentary on

[1] *ad Att.* I, 19, 2.
[2] *ad Q.F.* III, 1, 24.          [3] *ad fam.* XII, 15, 2.

the temptations which beset, and sometimes overcame, the governor, prove too that the Senate as a body was concerned for the welfare of the provinces and felt its responsibilities as an imperial power. The provinces may have been regarded as the estates of the Roman People, but the Senate, like a good landlord, realised that the most can only be got out of an estate if the tenants are prosperous. Again and again we find the Senate turning a sharp eye on the provincial governors. To say, as Jolliffe does, that the Senate looked on the provinces with 'haughty contempt' is a complete misrepresentation.

### FACTORS INFLUENCING SENATORIAL POLICY

The external policy of the Senate was dictated by many considerations. Every action was the result of several forces, some obvious, some latent. The Senate's only consistent motive was a desire for peace with honour, and a reluctance to increase its responsibilities. To understand its policy we must allow for many factors which were of slight import in themselves, but which were decisive in their cumulative effect.

#### Commercial interests

We have considered the influence of the Equites as a corporate body, and their relations with the Senate during this period. It is harder to determine how far the foreign policy of the Senate was affected by purely commercial motives. Tenney Frank concludes that the importance of this factor has been exaggerated, and that the part it played was very small.[1] Undoubtedly the

[1] *Op. cit.*; see bibliography.

historians of the last century overstressed the economic aspect of history, but we must not go too far in our reaction from them. Tenney Frank's arguments, moreover, are scarcely convincing; for most of them are merely negative, and the argument *de silentio* is never more fallacious than in Roman history. The pirate question provides him with his most telling point; for the half-hearted repression of these pests seems to him a proof that the Roman government was not seriously moved by danger to the trading class. But Heitland[1] actually derives an opposite conclusion from the same hypothesis. Commercial interests, he thinks, were the direct cause of Rome's delay; for many of the capitalist class were themselves financially interested in the pirates, through the medium of the Delian slave market, and naturally did not wish to queer their own pitch. Without accepting this argument, are we justified in building too much on the 'dilatoriness' of the Senate? It may have had to be 'prodded to action', but this was due rather to its innate caution than to any disregard for the trader; and once it did move it took energetic measures to repress the evil. As early as 139 a Roman embassy had been sent to several of the courts of the East to investigate the causes of the spread of piracy.[2] In 102 M. Antonius reduced the coast of Cilicia, the great haunt of pirates, and made it into a new province, while two years later a law of Marius declared that no toleration would be shown to pirates.[3] In 84 Murena commenced to

---

[1] *The Roman Republic*, sec. 804.          [2] Strabo, xiv, 634.

[3] This measure, which was probably not the subject of political controversy, has been preserved for us in an inscription at Delphi. Its main provision was that the allied princes and communities should be required

build up a fleet to pacify the sea, but his efforts were interrupted by the Second Mithridatic War.[1] From 78 to 74 M. Servilius Isauricus conducted some successful punitive expeditions in the highlands from which he took his name, and in the latter year M. Antonius (Creticus) received an extraordinary command to suppress the pirates. His failure was due not only to his own incompetence but to the death of L. Octavius, who was intended to co-operate with him on land. Finally the *Lex Gabinia*, which received considerable support in the Senate, was a determined effort to stamp out the practice.

Moreover, each provincial governor was expected to deal with the pirates as far as they came within his sphere; it is one of Cicero's gravest charges against Verres that he refused to do so. When supporting the *Lex Manilia*, Cicero exaggerates the evils of piracy to enhance Pompey's success, and we must not take his gloomy picture as correct. Piracy was not a sudden growth of the second century, but an endemic which fluctuated in virulence, and even Caesar was unable to stamp it out. Its survival does not presuppose an indifference to Roman commerce.

In actual fact, commercial interests played a large if unobtrusive part in the determination of foreign policy. By an old plebiscite of 218 senators were forbidden to engage in trade, but this law could easily be evaded,[2] and in one way or another many members of the Senate

---

to forbid the use of their territories to the pirates. See Supp. *Ep. Graec.* 3, 378; H. Stuart Jones, *J.R.S.* 1926, p. 155.

[1] *II in Verr.* 1, 35, 89.

[2] *V. supra*, p. 22 and note. Cf. also Kroll, *op. cit.* 1, 89 and references.

were interested in foreign commerce. Hence they could scarcely be indifferent to commercial and financial considerations.

'In Rome trade preceded rather than followed the flag.' We find Roman traders in Africa before the end of the Second Punic War. Caesar mentions the trade route over the Alps as a matter of course, while there was a similar route over the passes of the Pyrenees. A large number of the Italians massacred at Delos must, *pace* Mr Tenney Frank, have been Roman traders. The influence of commercial circles is shown by Cicero in his speech on the Manilian Law, where he speaks of the danger to the traders in Asia, and of the financial interests involved.[1] Similarly, when his brother Quintus consults him about the position of the bonded warehouses, he replies that he must consult the interests of 'the whole of Asia and the business world'.[2]

Even more important than the legitimate traders were the *negotiatores* or financial agents; although the term sometimes had the wider meaning of business men in general. Usually however the 'negotiator' was a Roman capitalist who played the same part in relation to the princes, cities, and individuals of the empire as Jew Süss did to the potentates of his day; but while the latter was only tolerated on sufferance, the former had the whole weight and majesty of Rome behind him. We

[1] Cf. Charlesworth, *Trade Routes and Commerce of the Roman Empire*, p. 76: 'When the strange whim of a half-insane king led him to bequeath his kingdom to the Romans, and a province of Asia had been created, merchants, dealers and traders of all kinds, finding a profitable field open for their labours, flocked in and overran the province.'

[2] Appian, *Hisp.* 4; Caesar, *b.g.* iii, 1; App. *Mith.* v, 28; Caesar, *b.g.* ii, 15; *de imp. Cn. Pomp.* 2, 6; 7, 18; *ad Att.* ii, 16, 4.

find these *negotiatores* in Gaul and Africa.[1] The exploits of Cn. Calidius in Sicily are known to us from the invective of Cicero. P. Sittius went to Spain as a moneylender and turned into a condottiere. The gentle Atticus had large interests in Macedonia. One small city, Nicaea, owed Pinnius, a Roman capitalist, £80,000. Asia was because of its wealth more honey-combed with the activities of these gentry than any other province. The ramifications of Roman capital in Asia were so vast that the collapse of the province caused a serious financial crisis at Rome.[2]

The occupation of the Balearic Isles in 123 by Q. Metellus, a firm supporter of the senatorial oligarchy, is significant. These were situated on the sea-route to Spain, and would form an *entrepôt* for the West in the same way as Delos did for the East. The military qualities of the natives would scarcely have provided sufficient stimulus, and Metellus was probably influenced at least in part by commercial considerations. Of the two colonies founded shortly afterwards in Majorca, many of the settlers were Roman citizens from Spain; these were in all likelihood traders.[3] Commercial interests too were largely responsible for the despatch of Pompey to the East. He not only re-established the security of the

[1] *pro Font.* 1, 11; Sall. *Jug.* 65.

[2] *II in Verr.* IV, 20, 42 ff.; *pro Sulla*, 20, 56 ff.; *ad Att.* III, 1, 1; *ad fam.* XIII, 61; *de imp. Cn. Pomp.* 7, 19. The extent of the Roman interests in Asia, even before the time of Sulla, is discussed by Tenney Frank (*An Economic Survey of Rome*, I, 277–8). Even if the eighty thousand 'citizens' slain by Mithridates on entering the province were mainly Italian rather than Roman, a large proportion of them were probably the local agents of the Equites.

[3] Strabo, III, 168.

Asiatic markets, but attempted to open up new avenues for Roman commerce. He even projected an expedition to Petra, the centre of the perfume and spice trade. The rapid influx of Roman traders into the new province of Syria is shown by the energetic steps which they took to protect themselves in 48, when they joined with the citizens of Antioch to fortify the Capitol. Athenodorus mentions a Roman colony at Petra before the end of the century.[1]

In 54 came Crassus' expedition to Parthia. Was he merely seeking to refurbish his tarnished military laurels, or is it possible, as Dr Giles has suggested,[2] that he was seeking to control the silk-routes to the East? The evidence is insufficient and Charlesworth refutes the suggestion; but it is quite possible that the arch-financier had less defined ambitions of opening up new fields for Roman trade.[3] Caesar's expedition to Britain was accompanied, if not inspired, by similar hopes. Cicero writes in jest to Trebatius that he hears there is neither gold nor silver in Britain. The Cassiterides, or Tin Isles, had long been known to Roman traders, but all they could find in Britain itself was pearls and slaves. They were compensated however by the rich new territories opened up to them in Gaul, which soon became as full of Roman traders and financiers as the other provinces.

## Party politics

There were no clear-cut parties in Roman politics, but at times the rivalry of the Senate, the People, and the

[1] Caesar, *bell. civ.* III, 102; Strabo, XVI, 779.

[2] *Proceedings Cambridge Philol. Soc.* 1929, p. 1.

[3] See article on Parthia by Tarn (*C.A.H.* IX). Crassus' main motive was undoubtedly his desire for military glory.

popular leaders had a vital bearing on foreign policy. External affairs were used as a pawn in the fight for supremacy at Rome, and were radically affected by 'party' manœuvres in the capital.

The treatment of Phrygia provides one of the first instances of the interference of the 'democratic party' in foreign policy, for it was C. Gracchus who opposed Aufeius' bill which was to confirm the grant of the country to Mithridates; in so doing he was probably angling for Equestrian support. The Senate, on principle, refused directly to annex Phrygia, and it remained for some years in loose dependence on the governor of Asia. The influence of 'party' appears too in the refusal of the Senate to take over Numidia in 50.[1] The senatorial proposal to recognise the king was vetoed by the optimate Marcellus—for personal reasons—but the Senate succeeded in blocking Curio's motion for annexation. Its motive was undoubtedly a wish to secure Juba's services for itself in the impending civil war.

A strange example of political intrigue is seen in the Eastern Expedition of Flaccus and Fimbria in 87. Ostensibly this was directed against Mithridates, but its real aim was the destruction of Sulla. Unfortunately their soldiers preferred to fight the barbarian rather than the Roman, and eventually most of them deserted and joined Sulla. For some time however there was the Gilbertian situation of two Roman armies fighting the same enemy, and at the same time hostile to one another. It was the difficulty of this position that led Sulla to offer Mithridates such favourable terms of peace at Dardanus.

[1] Caesar, *bell. civ.* ii, 25, 4.

A similar conflict of authority, but marred by less violence, occurred in Crete. In 71 the Cretans had forced Antonius to make a humiliating peace, and they had later sent an embassy to Rome to ask for friendship. Their request was blocked by a tribune, and the Senate sent out the consul for 69, Q. Caecilius Metellus, to reduce the island. Pompey was at this time pacifying the Mediterranean under the terms of the *Lex Gabinia*, and hearing of his moderation the Cretans sent envoys to make their surrender to him rather than to Metellus. Since no part of Crete was more than fifty miles from the sea, Pompey enjoyed his anomalous *imperium* over the whole island. He unwisely chose to assert his powers, and sent an officer Octavius to annex the island in his name. Metellus, a staunch senatorian, did not brook this interference and a minor civil war arose which was only brought to an end by the recall of Octavius. This incident was largely responsible for the opposition of the extreme senators to the *Lex Manilia* of the following year.

The appointment of Cn. Calpurnius Piso as *quaestor pro praetore* of Hither Spain in 65 was due to 'party' intrigue. Piso's lack of experience, and the part he had played in the First Catilinarian Conspiracy, support Sallust's suggestion[1] that he was a tool in the hands of Crassus, who was seeking to build up a power to counterbalance the growing influence of Pompey. It is scarcely credible that 'the Senate wished such a terrible fellow at a safe distance' (*ib.*); probably there were enough senators who shared Crassus' fear of Pompey to push the appointment through. The plan failed through the

[1] *Cat.* 19, 1.

incompetence of Piso, and on his death Crassus made no attempt to secure the appointment of a more reliable agent; for we have no reason to think that Sittius, the free-lance whom we have mentioned above, was acting under his auspices.[1] By 65, Crassus had another iron in the fire. He was hankering after the annexation of Egypt and was no longer interested in Spain. This step was opposed, however, by the more extreme senators under Catulus, who mistrusted any form of expansionist policy, and by Cicero, in the interests of his absent hero, and for the time being the plan was dropped.

The culminating example of the effect of party intrigue on external affairs is seen in the machinations of the Senate against Caesar, and the efforts to procure his recall. The struggle affected the other provinces too, for Curio's use of the veto to prevent one-sided proceedings against Caesar resulted in the postponement of all provincial appointments. What was of more importance to Cicero was that these intrigues caused his request for a *supplicatio* to be blocked. To us they are interesting as showing the extent to which 'party' feeling encroached on the interests of the State.

## *The personal factor*

The individual was always of supreme importance in Roman politics. Sometimes, as in the case of the Triumvirs, the individual acquired such a following that in his own person he represented a 'party'; when for instance the Senate attacks Caesar, we must distinguish whether

[1] Cf. Sall. *Cat.* 21, 3: (*Catilina dixit*) *esse in Hispania citeriore Pisonem, in Mauretania cum exercitu P. Sittium, consili sui participes*—and Cicero's defence of him, *pro Sulla*, 20, 56–9.

it is intriguing against him personally, or against the 'popular' ideas which he claimed to represent.

Münzer[1] suggests that the condemnation of Rutilius Rufus in 92 was largely due to the feud between the Caepiones and his own family. This is uncertain, but it is true that the prosecutor in many of the famous cases of the day was a known enemy of the defendant; and a governor was often accused of extortion through personal ill-will.

As will be seen, the personal factor played a large rôle in the rise and fall of Lucullus. We may note here that the *Lex Manilia* which led to his recall was strongly opposed by all his family connections, who rightly saw in it, despite the disclaimers of Cicero, a personal attack on their kinsman. It was supported on the other hand by Isauricus simply because of his hereditary and personal ill-will towards Lucullus.[2]

The bill was passed for the benefit of Pompey. Nor was he content merely to supersede other commanders. His attempts to deprive Marcius Rex, Metellus Creticus, and Lucullus himself, of their triumphs seem to us extraordinarily petty, but were quite in accordance with the conventions of Roman public life. He was to pay for this jealous attitude. Metellus became a leader of the senatorial opposition, and it was Lucullus who persuaded the Senate not to confirm Pompey's *acta en bloc*. Pompey also quarrelled with Cato, whose refusal of his proffered marriage alliance in 61 led to a deep rift between the two. This domestic quarrel was of far-reaching importance, for it helped to throw Pompey into the arms of Caesar and Crassus.

[1] *Op. cit.* p. 299.      [2] Cf. *de prov. cons.* 9, 22.

Caesar too incurred many enmities. Catulus' defeat in the pontifical elections was a severe blow to his pride, and he henceforth cherished a deep hostility towards his younger rival. Perhaps his influence is to be seen in the action of the Senate in originally earmarking a province of slight importance for the consuls of 59. The staunch constitutionalist Cato detested Caesar as a revolutionary. Hignett[1] rather unkindly suggests that his proposal to surrender him to the Germans was due as much to political antipathy as to genuine indignation.

The Egyptian imbroglio brought a crop of motives into play. It led too to a recrudescence of the rivalry between Pompey and Crassus. The pair had always been jealous of one another, and only the personal influence of Caesar had kept them together. As yet he dared not allow the Triumvirate to dissolve; hence it was re-cemented at Lucca. But Pompey gradually drew farther from his allies, and his marriage connection with the Metelli openly marked his new orientation. Indeed, throughout this period the marriage alliances of the great leaders were of as much political importance as those of the seventeenth-century dynasts.

### Imperialism

Tenney Frank has investigated at length the question of Roman Imperialism.[2] It is now generally accepted that the expansion of Rome was due rather to force of circumstances than to any preconceived plan; it is diffi-cult to find any traces of a consistent expansionist

[1] *C.A.H.* IX, 599; but as Adcock (*ib.* 620) speaks of Cato's 'rare courage' in taking such a step, we may assume that the *Cambridge Ancient History* does not condemn it whole-heartedly.

[2] *Roman Imperialism* (see bibliography).

policy. Arnold suggests that after the remission of the tribute in 167 the 'lust for conquest' entered into the Roman People, but there is little evidence for this. Tenney Frank too postulates that it was usually the 'democratic' party at Rome which favoured a policy of expansion. It is true that a popular assembly tends to be chauvinistic but the Roman People was in general more interested in the exploitation of the provinces it already possessed than in the acquisition of new ones. Nor must we suppose that the average Eques was an active expansionist. His scope was not confined to Roman territory, and, as Stevenson[1] suggests, his profits may well have been still larger in a client kingdom, where he was not under the eye of a Roman governor.

If the People and the Equites were lukewarm, the Senate was actively opposed to a policy of expansion. There was no standing army and it was dangerous to entrust troops to an ambitious general. The Senate never annexed new territory except where military or economic reasons made it inevitable. The demand for a settlement with Jugurtha was due to the losses of the Roman traders, not to a desire for land. The recall of Lucullus was facilitated by mistrust of his forward policy in the East.[2] The Parthian expedition was equally unpopular at Rome, as is shown by the melodramatic behaviour of the tribune Ateius Capito; Crassus had to resort to conscription to muster an army. Mithridates'

[1] *C.A.H.* IX, 440.

[2] In reality Lucullus upheld the orthodox policy of the Senate: his desire for 'empire and riches' (Plut. *Luc.* 33) was a canard spread by the Equites (*v. inf.* p. 119).

statement in his letter to Phraates that the Roman's sole motive for war was a 'profound lust for rule and riches' was designed merely to awaken the fears of the Parthian.[1] The popular demand for the annexation of Egypt, an apparent exception to these conclusions, was due more to sheer desire for wealth than to any deep-seated imperialism.[2]

For a deliberate policy of expansion we have to wait for the Triumvirs; and even Pompey can scarcely be called an imperialist. If it is too much to say that 'he never had a policy of his own',[3] it is true that he had no broad vision of empire. His settlement of Asia was dictated by sound practical considerations, but he deliberately shirked the more important questions at issue. He maintained the old system of 'dependence rather than incorporation', and he left the Parthian problem unsolved, to be a pregnant source of trouble for a hundred years. It may be, as Dobiáš suggests, that he realised the essential weakness of Parthia; but at Rome at any rate the fears of a Parthian invasion continued to constitute a very real fear. His acquisitions of territory were due partly to the necessity for a safe frontier, partly to the army's demands for money and land, and above all to the exigencies of the pirate problem.

We may agree with Tenney Frank that Julius Caesar was the first candid imperialist of Rome, and that the Gallic War is the clearest instance of deliberate expansion in the history of the Republic. His methods betray a well-laid plan for the conquest and annexation

---

[1] Sall. *hist.* IV, 69 (Maurenbrecher).

[2] *de reg. Alex.* frag. A. xv, 7; *de leg. agr.* II, 16, 42.

[3] Tenney Frank, *Roman Imperialism*, p. 316.

of the whole country. The Senate approved of his conquests because it realised that a forward policy was often
the best, indeed the only, method of defence; and fired
by his exploits it began for the first time to contemplate
the possibility of expansion and conquest for its own
sake.[1]

Two other factors which affected the foreign policy
of Rome were:

## A. *The corn supply*

Sulla had shown his appreciation of the importance of
this in 83, by his prompt seizure of Sardinia, Sicily and
Africa. These were the granaries of Rome, for Egypt
was as yet a practically untouched market. In 75 the
scarcity and high price of corn almost provoked a riot,
and two years later the *Lex Terentia Cassia* had to be
passed to accelerate the flow of corn from Sicily to
Rome. At the same time, by introducing the cheap corn
dole once more, it made the corn supply a political
question. Antonius' command against the pirates in 74
was largely due to the havoc they wrought upon the corn
fleets, while the election of Cornelius and Gabinius as
tribunes in 67, and their resulting activity, was dictated
by the popular discontent at the corn shortage. It was
the prospect of a hungry mob that led the Senate to
decisive action to safeguard the corn supply ten years
later. Clodius suggested that this shortage was due to
Pompey's machinations, but it is easier to believe Cicero's
explanation which attributes it to scarcity of crops,
commercial speculation, and a desire on the part of
the provinces to keep supplies back until prices were

[1] *de prov. cons.* 13, 32.

high.[1] On his proposal the Senate conferred special powers on Pompey, to purchase corn and charter transport for five years; this early instance of 'rationalisation' was brilliantly successful.

## B. *Finance*

Rome had no scientifically regulated annual budget, and the Treasury existed from hand to mouth. The income from the provinces was scarcely sufficient to make up for the remission of internal taxation and the increased expenditure on administration. The cost of what we should term 'social services' was as yet small, but it was growing: in the introduction of the corn dole we see the beginnings of the vast eleemosynary projects of the Empire. Hence the prospect of financial shortage was never remote, and the Senate was confirmed in its policy of peace and retrenchment. In 75 the wars in Asia, Macedonia and Spain proved such a drain on the Treasury that the State was threatened with bankruptcy. The same fear appears repeatedly in Cicero's speeches. In supporting the *Lex Manilia* he stresses the financial motive and makes the tribute one of the stakes at issue. It is a damning charge against Gabinius that by not assisting the tax-farmers he had added to the burden of the Treasury at a difficult time; and Cicero adduces its grant to Caesar as a proof of its generosity in spite of its straitened means. Perhaps one of Clodius' more honourable motives for the annexation of Cyprus was a desire to enrich the Treasury.[2] In the following

[1] *ap.* Plut. *Pomp.* 49; *de dom.* 5, 11. Cicero discreetly veils the identity of the speculators responsible for the shortage: we may suspect Roman capitalists.

[2] Amm. Marc. I, 8.

year Cicero can declare outright that the resources of the State are used up.[1]

The conclusions to be drawn from this survey may be summarised as follows:

1. The force of public opinion in controlling the affairs of Rome has been exaggerated.

2. There was little conscious imperialism in any class.

3. Purely commercial interests existed, but must not be overstressed at this period.

4. Shortage of money, absence of a permanent civil service, and fear of the 'great general' acted as a constant deterrent to expansion.

5. The main factors affecting the policy of the Senate were the financial interests represented by the Equites, and the personal rivalries of the leading statesmen of the day.

## THE FOREIGN POLICY OF THE SENATE

The above considerations enable the broad outlines of a senatorial policy to be formulated. The Senate had not sought to become an imperial power, but it was resolved to rule the provinces soundly and efficiently. Administration could not be centralised beyond a certain point, but it was essential to prevent any one governor acquiring too much power. Hence the system of yearly commands and the numerous checks on a governor's freedom of action.

For financial and political reasons war, and especially war of aggression, was to be avoided. The peace of the

[1] *de harus.* 27. 60.

provinces demanded a strong frontier; since the Senate
had neither the money nor the wish to maintain a large
frontier force, this necessitated that system of buffer-
states which became a fixed principle of Roman policy.
It was an old-established axiom that victory in war
confirmed the sovereignty of Rome,[1] but this principle
was often neglected; Lucullus' attempted restoration of
a Seleucid to the throne of Syria was in the sound Sullan
tradition. This system of 'client-princeship' was
buttressed by the principle that no strong State should
be allowed to grow up on the frontier. When Mithridates increased his realm by the partition of Cappadocia
and Paphlagonia, Sulla was sent to restore Ariobarzanes
(92). The fear of a German invasion led to vigorous
measures for the protection of Gaul in 60. Crassus'
Eastern Expedition was grudgingly countenanced because of the fear felt by the Senate for Parthia. The
problem was complicated by the fact that the frontiers
were in many cases unsatisfactory; Rome had not yet
reached the natural boundaries of her Empire.

Inside the provinces the Senate's aim was simple; to
maintain the interests of its own citizens, and hence,
indirectly, of the natives, with the minimum of interference and expense. Local institutions were left as far
as possible untouched. To maintain its supremacy, and
to limit the field of ambitious governors, the Senate
firmly adhered to the principle of *divide et impera*.
Political leagues were disbanded or made non-political.
The Achaian League, for instance, had been broken up

[1] Cf. Pompey's annexation of Syria after the defeat of Tigranes, and
Caesar's rather sophistical claim to Gaul on the grounds of the victory
over the Arverni in 121.

in 146; the leagues of Sicily and Lycia were allowed to
remain shorn of their political power. New assize
divisions were made which disregarded and cut across
race distinctions.[1]  Differences of privilege and land
tenure were instituted; sometimes, as in the case of
Macedonia, a country was arbitrarily split up. Joint
action was encouraged neither between municipalities,
nor, in a larger field, between provinces.

The critical state of domestic politics had great bearing
upon the foreign policy of Rome. It intensified the
natural caution of the Senate, for obviously the time was
unripe for a forward policy. The political influence of
the Equites resulted in their representatives, the local
*publicani*, being treated with a consideration which they
did not deserve. The ambition of the local leaders made
the Senate chary of trusting any governor with too much
power. Considerations of practical necessity combined
with the intrigues of the Triumvirs to compel the Senate
to reverse its own policy by the institution of extraordinary commands, which were finally to lead to the
downfall of the Republic. The system of 'client-prince-
dom' fell into disrepute owing to the mass of corruption
which accrued to it. The ambition of Caesar, whether a
desire for personal glory, or something higher, could
not accommodate itself to the cautious policy of retrenchment advocated by the Senate. The Roman People,
enervated by a life of idleness in the capital, refused to
play their part in the government of the world by serving
in a citizen army for the duration of a campaign before
returning quietly to civilian life. It was when the Roman

[1] Cf. Strabo, xiii, 629: 'The Romans added to the confusion (in Asia)
by not making the circuit divisions according to tribes, but otherwise.'

soldier began to look to his general for large donatives and grants of land that the senatorial system of foreign and provincial administration began to sag.

## ROME AND THE CLIENT-PRINCES

Roman foreign policy, as we have pointed out, centred round the 'client-prince'. The buffer-state has always been a recognised institution of imperial diplomacy, and it relieved Rome from the necessity of a strong defence force. The whole purpose of client-kingship, from the Roman point of view, is embraced in a sentence of the *Bellum Alexandrinum—provincias populi Romani barbaris atque inimicis regibus interposito amicissimo rege munivit.*[1] Sands, in his *Client-Princes of the Roman Empire*, has dealt at length with the functions, duties and privileges of the princes; here it will be sufficient to touch upon the general policy of the Senate towards them. In judging it we must not be influenced by the modern attitude towards protected and mandated territory. The Senate did not feel that it had a mission to Romanise the border states of the Empire; the system of client-princeship was evolved as a practical method of securing the frontier, and was a business agreement from first to last.

1. The guiding principle of the Senate was that its supremacy must be maintained. Hence Sulla rejected Mithridates' offer of help in 84 when he was returning from Dardanus; similarly Sertorius never forgot that it was as a Roman magistrate that he negotiated with Mithridates, and he refused to surrender to him any of the Roman provinces. This superiority was fostered by

[1] § 78. Cf. Tacitus, *Agric.* 14: *ut haberet instrumenta servitutis et reges.*

the servility of many of the princes. The humble de-
meanour of Masinissa and Adherbal was imitated by
the kings of the East.[1]

2. The main aim of Rome was to keep the peace.
Hence the kings were supposed to submit their quarrels
to the arbitration of the Senate. If a client were attacked
he could appeal to Rome for help, and a vote of the Senate
might be passed in his favour. Sulla assisted Ariobarzanes I against Mithridates in 92; Caesar sent aid to
Deiotarus and Ariobarzanes III against Pharnaces in
47. Usually permission from Rome had to be obtained
before a governor could help a neighbouring prince.
Thus Pompey refused to help Tigranes against Pharnaces on the ground that he had no authority. It was
exceptional when Caesar in his first consulship sent aid
to kings without consulting the Senate.

Gabinius left a contingent of Gauls and Germans in
Egypt—ostensibly to protect the king, but perhaps also
to look after his own interests.[2] He was also charged
by Cicero with 'hiring out' troops to Ariobarzanes like
a Thracian condottiere.[3] Cicero lent a small body of
troops to Deiotarus to form the nucleus of a new army.
Herod was established by Roman troops and had a legion
left to support him. Most interesting is the help sent
by Cicero to Ariobarzanes. It was essential that Cappadocia should be in strong and loyal hands. He established
the king more firmly on his throne by the firm suppression of an incipient revolt, and then lent him troops
with the special authorisation of the Senate.[4] 'The king
asked for cavalry and some companies from my army,'

[1] Livy, XLV, 13; Sallust, *Jug.* XIV, 1.
[2] Caesar, *bell. civ.* III, 4.
[3] *de prov. cons.* 4, 9.
[4] *ad fam.* XV, 2, 7.

he writes, ' . . . I knew that by decree of the Senate I not only might but ought to grant his request.'

3. Internally the Romans did not interfere unless it was necessary to preserve the stability of the realm. The client-kingdoms were outside the Roman *imperium* and hence no magistrate could enter them on his own authority. Caesar roused a riot at Alexandria merely by entering it with the lictors of a magistrate.

This policy of non-intervention laid Rome open, with some justice, to the charge of neglecting the welfare of her clients' subjects; but the Senate was only in part responsible for the misery that prevailed among the native peoples. Many of the Asiatic kingdoms were in a bad state as a result of centuries of warfare. Bithynia may have been overrun by Roman traders and slave dealers, but these can only have accentuated the distress of the country. Nor can the condition of Cappadocia in 51 be attributed solely to the machinations of Roman financiers.[1] The cause lay rather in the inefficient administration of the kingdoms. Until Appius advised Ariobarzanes to lay a tribute on his subjects to pay his debts the royal treasury had had no regular income. Such interference was rare until Augustus reversed the policy of the Senate, and embarked on a policy of systematic intervention in client-kingdoms.

4. It follows that the annexation of a client-kingdom was unpopular and was postponed as long as possible. The Senate had no large standing army to take over the defence of the frontier from the princes. The Treasury could not stand the additional strain of administrating these bankrupt kingdoms. Cicero, speaking on the

[1] Diod. xxxvi, 1; *ad Att.* vi, 1, 3.

Egyptian question, condemned attempts to extend sovereignty over the client-princes; elsewhere he reproves the popular desire to annex Egypt merely for the sake of the immediate loot.[1] The average protectorate offered less prospect of gain and was not coveted by any party in the State.

The Roman policy is well illustrated by the history of the Aedui. This Gallic tribe had been formally recognised as friends and allies of the Roman people in 121, because of the support given to Rome against the Allobroges and the Arverni. The alliance was renewed after the overthrow of the Cimbri and Teutones, but the Senate took no step towards annexation. Even when the Aedui appealed for help against Ariovistus in 61, the Senate merely commended their allies' interests to the governor of Transalpine Gaul in deliberately vague terms; if it had desired to pursue a forward policy, this would have been an excellent opportunity to assert direct suzerainty over central Gaul. The recognition of Ariovistus in 59 did not affect the relations between Rome and the Aedui, for its implications were personal rather than territorial. It was left for Caesar, 'the first imperialist', to incorporate the Aedui in the Empire. Their participation in the revolt of Gaul gave him sufficient pretext, if any were needed, for annexation, and this marked the end of an alliance which had lasted for over sixty years.

[1] *de reg. Alex.* frag. A, xv, 7; *de leg. agr.* ii, 16, 42.

## ANNEXATION

Such an unequal alliance was however bound to merge into empire eventually. The usual occasion for annexation was the death of a king; as the grant of the title was personal, Rome could withhold recognition from his successor and take over the kingdom. But such a step was unpopular in the Senate if there were any suitable candidate for the vacant throne. Clodius' action in persuading the Assembly to depose Ptolemy of Cyprus met with its strong disapproval; and Cicero later drew a pathetic picture of the monarch 'coming up for auction' regalia and all.[1]

Annexation also followed a bequest by the last king in Rome's favour. Rostovtzeff asserts that 'the testaments of client-kings were for a while a device in the foreign policy of the ruling party in the Roman Senate, a kind of disguised imperialism', and Cary compares Lord Auckland's policy of 'lapse' in India. There is no need for this supposition, which is directly opposed to our view of the policy of the Senate. In every instance of an accepted bequest, as Sands points out, the testator was the last of his race, dying childless; and what was more natural than that the dying monarch should voluntarily 'surrender his kingdom to the full control of the power which had for so long wielded an indirect sovereignty'?[2]

An inscription recently discovered at Cyrene, which records the testament of Ptolemy Neoteros, and is prob-

[1] *pro Sest.* 26, 57.

[2] *C.A.H.* IX, 226; Sands, *op. cit.* pp. 145 ff.; cf. Arnold, *Roman Provincial Administration*, p. 11: 'That it was not really independent and powerful monarchs who so acted is obvious.'

ably to be assigned to the year 156, provides us with the first example of such a bequest. As Ptolemy was at this time only about thirty years of age there seems to be an ulterior motive behind this public statement of his wish that, should his heirs fail, his kingdom shall fall to the Roman People. F. E. Adcock well suggests that Ptolemy may have hoped both to impress Rome with his fidelity and to warn his restless subjects that a revolt might lead to annexation. The bequest was, in fact, a diplomatic move, and it did not come into force: it is important for us as showing that Rome was already regarded as the *deus ex machina* who might intervene to settle the complicated politics of the Hellenistic world.[1]

Enemies of Rome disputed the genuineness of the will of Attalus of Pergamum, whose bequest was the first to become valid, but an inscription has proved it to be a real testament;[2] that the bequest was accepted so quickly was due to the precipitancy of Tiberius Gracchus, not the Senate. The validity of the wills of Nicomedes of Bithynia and Ptolemy Apion of Cyrene is well established. The fact that Cyrene was not made a province for twenty years, although the silphium monopoly and the royal domains were taken over straight away, seems to prove that the bequest was unforced. The only case of a doubtful bequest was that of Egypt. Perhaps, as Sands sug-

[1] For this inscription see De Sanctis, *Riv. Fil.* LX, 59 ff.; M. N. Tod, *J.H.S.* 1933, p. 263; Scullard, *A History of the Roman World, 753–146 B.C.*, p. 302; F. E. Adcock (*Proc. Camb. Phil. Soc.*), *C.U. Reporter*, LXII, p. 1290.

[2] Adcock (*op. cit., supra*) suggests that Attalus may have been influenced by the same motives as Ptolemy Neoteros, and that 'the accident of his death by sunstroke may have converted a gesture of appeal to Rome and to the citizens of Pergamum into a gesture of renunciation'.

gests, the rumour of the will was originated by Sulla. He did nothing, however, except seize the royal treasure at Tyre; further intervention was directly opposed by Catulus and Hortensius, and the latter even insisted on the recognition of Ptolemy Auletes. In none of these cases is it possible to regard the will of the last king as an instrument of 'senatorial imperialism'.

Where annexation was inevitable, whether as a result of inheritance or conquest, the policy of the Senate was the same. Full ownership was asserted over the former royal estates, and the rest of the land was left to its possessors. There was nothing to prevent Rome asserting her rights of ownership over the whole land, but such a step was scarcely contemplated by the Senate. Its aim was to disturb the existing tenure of land as little as possible, and hence it was content with political *dominium* alone.

## Egypt

The system of clientship was open to one grave abuse. Since recognition by the Senate was of such importance to a prince, it was worth his while to cultivate powerful friends at Rome. The sad fate of Ptolemy of Cyprus shows that a prince dare not neglect to secure the good-will of men of influence in the capital. As Cicero himself confesses 'It is no virtue for a king to be accounted frugal.'[1] The responsibility for this state of affairs rests not so much with the Senate as with the popular leaders whom it was powerless to restrain. Supporters of the old régime might abhor the shameless trafficking of the magistrates but they could do little to stop it; nor was

[1] *pro reg. Deiot.* 9, 26.

the Senate itself above suspicion in this matter. The activities of Caesar, Vatinius and Clodius have been mentioned above;[1] but the special case of Egypt deserves lengthier treatment. The wealth and fertility of the country gave it great importance in Roman eyes, while the 'Egyptian question' and its developments dominated domestic politics at Rome for some years.

Ptolemy Alexander, king of Egypt, died in 80 B.C. after making a will in favour of Rome; but even Cicero dare not assert the existence of the testament as a fact. As we have seen, the Senate took no steps to accept the 'bequest' and it was proposed that one of the claimants to the vacant throne should be recognised. The task of establishing or restoring a Ptolemy offered endless scope to an ambitious general. The wealth of Egypt was proverbial, and presumably the king would not prove ungrateful. The Piper Prince who sat precariously on the throne was certainly eager for Roman support; Cicero mentions in his letters the activity displayed at Rome by his agents.[2]

In 66 Caesar was intriguing to be entrusted with the task of establishing Auletes.[3] His attempt to gain his ends by a *plebiscitum* fell through, owing to the opposition of the People. This was not, as Sands suggests,[4] a 'popular outcry against regal mismanagement', but was due rather to sheer greed. The Roman People wanted to increase the bounds of the empire no more than the Senate; but in its desire for wealth it grudged seeing

---

[1] *V. supra*, pp. 16–17; see also Jolliffe, *Phases of Corruption in Roman Administration*.

[2] *ad fam.* I, 1, 1.

[3] Suet. *Jul.* 11; Ferrero rejects this, but his arguments are unconvincing.                    [4] *Op. cit.* p. 159 n.

the riches of Egypt fall once more under the control of an all but independent king. On the other hand, Crassus' proposal, by means of a friendly tribune, that he should be sent out to annex the country, was rejected through the influence of Catulus and Cicero. Crassus was obviously seeking to build up a military power in the East to counterbalance that of Pompey; Cicero was alert to defend the interests of his absent friend and hero; while Catulus was merely upholding the senatorial doctrine of non-interference.

Egypt was also scheduled for annexation in the agrarian proposals of Rullus. The measure was quashed, and in 59 Caesar at last succeeded in getting Ptolemy acknowledged as 'king and friend of the Roman People'. The market price for this service was 6000 talents which was probably divided between Caesar and Pompey. An embassy to the king was mooted, but does not seem to have materialised.[1]

In 57 the king once more found himself in need of help, for the Alexandrians had risen in revolt and driven him out of his kingdom. The Senate had no wish to entrust his restoration to one of the Triumvirs, and the consul Lentulus Spinther received the commission. Suddenly an oracle was discovered in the Sibylline Books forbidding the restoration of the Egyptian king by means of an army, and the question was re-opened. The Senate seized hold of this suspiciously opportune oracle, and declared that Roman intervention must only be diplomatic. Hortensius, supported by Cicero, still

[1] Apparently the king had gradually consolidated his position on the throne by his own efforts; in 63 he had been able to send 8000 cavalry to Pompey.

pressed the claims of Lentulus. Bibulus advocated putting
the authority into commission between three legates.
Crassus was working behind the scenes for himself.
Pompey was outwardly in favour of Lentulus, but
Cicero suspected that he was angling for support for his
own claims. It was a state of deadlock; and once again
the matter was shelved.[1]

It seems probable that a plan for Ptolemy's restoration was discussed at Lucca, and that, as Dio states,[2]
Pompey sent Gabinius, the governor of Syria, instructions to restore the king, by force if necessary. In 54
Gabinius entered Egypt and fulfilled this commission.
He was most reluctant to give up his province to the
deputy whom Crassus sent to take it over, and when he
did evacuate it he left a confidential agent, Rabirius, in
Egypt to safeguard his interests. He was greeted at
Rome with a storm of indignation. He was twice tried,
for treason and extortion, and he was exiled on the
latter charge despite the efforts of Pompey and Caesar
to save their tool. Pompey harangued the jurors himself, and prevailed on Cicero to undertake the defence.
In the light of these facts, Cicero's statement that
Gabinius acted on his own initiative is scarcely plausible.

As for Rabirius, he was a man after Gabinius' own
kidney. He was a prominent Roman financier, and he
willingly undertook the Egyptian commission because
he had himself lent money to Ptolemy as a long-term
investment. To ensure repayment of his own debts, and
of the 10,000 talents the king had promised Gabinius,
he insisted on being appointed Διοικήτης, or super-

[1] ad Q.F. ii, 2, 3; ad fam. i, 1, 3; Plut. Crass. 13.
[2] Dio, xxxix, 55.

intendent of the Treasury. With the support of Roman troops he commenced a systematic exploitation of the country, which eventually led, in the natural course of events, to a popular rising. Rabirius was compelled to leave the country in haste. Accused of corruption on his return to Rome in 53, he was defended by Cicero and acquitted; but he was only saved from bankruptcy by Caesar, who took over his claims on Ptolemy in return.[1]

The whole affair illustrates not only the persistent reluctance of the Senate to annex a client-kingdom, but also the corruption and self-seeking of the popular leaders, even the irreproachable Pompey. The condemnation of Gabinius is evidence too for the determination of the Senate to maintain its provincial regulations, and is a proof that even with the lax scale of public morality that prevailed, it was still impossible to overstep the mark too flagrantly with impunity.[2]

[1] For Rabirius, see Pauly-Wissowa, II, i, A. 1, 25.

[2] Gabinius had also incurred the hostility of the Equites (*v. supra*, p. 28). It was the influence of Senate and Equites combined that secured his conviction in the teeth of his powerful protectors.

## CHAPTER III

# THE APPOINTMENT OF THE PROVINCIAL GOVERNOR

DURING the second century before Christ the Senate had evolved a system of providing for the government of the provinces by means of the prorogation of the urban magistracies. The competition for command in the provinces helped to make the principle of annually changing the governor into a constitutional maxim. The Senate had a very large control over the appointments in that it decided which provinces should be consular and which praetorian, and it could prolong a governor's term of office at will. Its power was restricted by the *Lex Sempronia* which ordained that the consular provinces should always be named before the elections; but the Senate could easily anticipate the election of an opponent by naming two provinces of slight importance.[1] Moreover, the law expressly exempted the decision of the Senate from the veto of the tribune. Apparently even Gracchus realised that the ordinary routine of the 'Colonial Office' could not be subjected to the caprice of a popular magistrate.

On the other hand the ultimate authority of the People was firmly maintained. It was a *plebiscitum* of C. Man-

[1] In 59 the Senate discriminated against Caesar by naming two 'provinces of the least importance' (Suet. *Jul.* 19) as consular. These were not, as is often stated, *Silvae Callesque*: this was a purely civilian province, more appropriate to a quaestor, and is probably a gloss on the MS. of Suetonius.

lius which handed over Numidia to the consul Marius in 107. In 88 the *Lex Sulpicia* abrogated Sulla's *imperium* and appointed Marius proconsul of Asia. Sulla never forgave this slight, and when he returned to Rome he was determined to make a thorough re-organisation of the provincial arrangements.

## THE *LEX CORNELIA DE PROVINCIIS ORDINANDIS* (81 B.C.)

The outstanding achievement of this law was that it established a distinction between the civil magistrate and the urban pro-magistrate. Henceforth it is the custom for the former to exercise his *imperium* in Rome, the latter in the provinces. The many exceptions do not affect the general application of this rule.

Sulla recognised the right of the Senate to determine the consular and praetorian provinces, and to create special pro-magistracies, but even he could not impugn the right of the People in moments of crisis to take matters into its own hands and make a direct election to a pro-magistracy. In view of the popular commands given to Pompey and Caesar, Arnold has little ground for asserting that 'it became impossible for the comitia to give a man direct military command".[1]

One of the great merits of the Sullan system was its elasticity. This has caused difficulty to historians who have tried to fit every particular example into a Procrustean bed of general rules of their own making. The working of the system can only be appreciated if we allow for the flexibility which was an integral part of it.

[1] *Op. cit.* p. 50; Shuckburgh, in his revision, modifies this statement in a note.

The Senate had yearly to decree two consular and eight praetorian provinces; but these decisions were in no way connected, for they were concerned with different years. Thus, as Cicero shows in his speech 'On the Consular Provinces', in 56 the Senate had to decide on the praetorian provinces for 55 and the consular for 54. It was immaterial in what order the bills were passed, but the consular provinces were usually discussed first, as a decision had to be reached before the elections.

After the passing of the necessary *senatus consultum*, the praetors cast lots for their own provinces. Not all the provinces were vacated each year, as some praetors did not want a province, and abstained from the lot with the tacit approval of the Senate. In defending Murena, Cicero mentions that Sulpicius, like himself, had not taken up a province after his praetorship. Our records of provincial governors are scanty, but we know too that in 55 Milo and Vatinius refused provinces; in 54 Cato similarly elected to stay in Rome. Probably there was no allotment of provinces at all in 53, for Cassius, Appius and Attius remained unrelieved in Syria, Cilicia and Africa respectively, while L. Aemilius Paullus, the only praetor of whom we know, certainly stayed in the capital.

The consuls cast lots only if they could not come to an amicable agreement with each other.[1] Pompey's assertion that he would refuse to leave Rome for a province on the expiration of his consulship shows that by 70 the consuls were expected to proceed to an overseas command, but here again a magistrate who wished to stay in Rome could do so by arrangement with the Senate.

[1] *ad fam.* 1, 9, 25: *Appius dixit se paraturum cum collega.*

Cicero won over his colleague Antonius by resigning his claims on the wealthy province of Macedonia. Of the consuls for 56, Philippus certainly, and Marcellinus perhaps, did not take a province. In 54 Appius Claudius was allotted Cilicia, but L. Domitius Ahenobarbus stayed in Rome.

Perhaps, too, even where the consuls did not come to some agreement about the provinces, it was not unknown for one of them to tamper with the lot. Thus Cicero hints to his successor Q. Metellus Celer:[1] 'I say nothing about your casting lots; I only want you to realise that my colleague[2] has done nothing in this matter behind my back.' The Senate probably acquiesced in Metellus' faking of the lot for practical reasons, as the impending trouble in Gaul demanded a strong governor. It was the same motive that led it, on the motion of Cicero, to rescind the appointment of Pupius Piso as governor of Syria in 61, as he was an obviously unsuitable man for the position.[3] The Senate adapted the rules to meet the circumstances of the moment. Thus one of the consuls for 64 refused to take a province because he rightly thought the critical state of affairs demanded his presence in Rome.[4] In the same way it was a sound instinct that prompted Fannius' proposal in 50 that the governors should leave their provinces 'unless the Parthians assumed a hostile attitude before the month of July'; although the strict constitutionalist Cicero disliked the practical proviso.

[1] *ad fam.* v, 2, 3.
[2] Antonius, who would be in charge of the allotment of provinces.
[3] *ad. Att.* I, 16, 8: *desponsam homini Syriam ademi.*
[4] *de leg. agr.* I, 8, 26.

Although Sulla established the general rule that the magistrate should go to his province at the end of his year of office at Rome, he did not lay this down as a hard and fast regulation. Mommsen and Stahl seem to be wrong in stating that Sulla abolished the military command of the consuls, and forbade them to leave Rome during their term of office. Willems rightly maintains that 'the consuls at any rate were not compelled by law to stay their year in Rome. It only gradually grew to be the custom'.[1] It is probable that Metellus left for Spain before the end of his year of office in 80.[2] In 78 Lepidus and Catulus were given a military command in Etruria, and in 74 Lucullus and Cotta left for the East before the end of the summer. In 60, when the fear of a German invasion led the Senate to make the two Gauls consular provinces, it was probably prepared to send the consuls to the front before their magistracy had expired if the danger of the moment demanded it. Caesar left for Gaul during 58, Crassus for Parthia about the Ides of November, 55.[3] During the Parthian scare of 51 it was proposed in the Senate that the consuls for the year should be sent to the East immediately. Lentulus Spinther, too, left for his province of Cilicia before his year of office was up. Praetors also could be entrusted with military commands. In 74 M. Antonius left Italy for his campaign against the pirates while he was still praetor; two years later M. Crassus led out an army to reduce Spartacus.

There is a belief that Sulla intended to limit the tenure

[1] *Le Sénat de la République romaine*, ii, 578.
[2] Appian, *bell. civ.* i, 97.
[3] Cf. reference in Cicero's letters: *ad. Att.* iv, 13, 2.

of a provincial command strictly to one year. This is deduced from the fact that he increased the number of higher magistracies so that they were now exactly equal to the number of provinces; hence each year there were enough ex-magistrates to provide reliefs for all the provinces at once. But as we have seen, some of the magistrates might not wish to proceed to a command; and there is no evidence that Sulla contemplated increasing the number of magistracies to match the growth of the empire which he must have foreseen. The annual command may have been his rough ideal, but he made no attempt to tie the Senate's hands; the exceptions to this rule are many, even where there were no practical considerations to make a prolongation of command advisable. After Sulla's time the governor remained in power until the arrival of his successor without formal prorogation, and in the Ciceronian Age, as Stevenson points out,[1] three years seems to have been a very usual term of office. The example of Cicero himself shows that a governor sometimes had difficulty in securing relief at the end of his year of office; despite his prayers for recall, Hortensius actually proposed that he should be left in Cilicia for another year.

When Cicero attributes Lucullus' recall to the constitutional aversion to long commands he deceived nobody. Lucullus' eight years in Asia were unique in degree but not in principle. P. Servilius Isauricus had been five years, 78–74, in Cilicia.[2] Even before the reforms of Sulla, Sentius had governed Macedonia from

[1] *C.A.H.* I, 453; cf. also Last, *ib.* p. 295.
[2] *II in Verr.* III, 90, 211: *quinquennium*. He was not relieved by Octavius, the consul for 75, until the late summer of 74.

92 to 88. Murena held Asia from 84 to 82; Q. Cicero spent three years in the same province. The three years of Cosconius in Illyricum (78–75) can have been due neither to his outstanding ability nor to the critical situation of the province; Verres' similar term of office shows that it was not only good governors who had their commands prolonged. Fonteius was three years in Transalpine Gaul; it seems that he left for his province during his praetorship. Such long commands were exceptionally common during the closing years of the Republic, for political intrigue at Rome often delayed or prevented the discussion of the provincial arrangements. Lentulus Spinther was in Cilicia from 56 to 53. In 51 Caelius warned Cicero that the deadlock with regard to Caesar's recall might block the whole of the provincial appointments; this actually happened the following year.

This tendency was accelerated by the course of domestic politics, but it was essentially practical. When Caesar strictly limited the tenure of office to two years for a proconsul and one for a propraetor he was taking a retrograde step which 'sacrificed the provincial to the security of the home government'.[1] One of the many admirable points of Tiberius' much-criticised administration was his restoration of the system of long commands.

A governor's appointment was usually confirmed before he left Rome by an individual *lex curiata de imperio,* in accordance with the custom by which only the curiate assembly could grant *imperium.* Was this law indispensable or merely desirable? It could be maintained

[1] Adcock, *C.A.H.* ix, 698.

that the *Lex Cornelia* sufficed to grant authority to a governor. Mommsen inclines towards this view, but is less dogmatic than usual.[1] Rullus' agrarian bill provided that the authority of the commissioners should not be impaired by the absence of a *lex curiata*; Cicero attacks this proposal, and upholds the authority of the curiate law, but he does not categorically condemn the exception.[2]

In 54 the *lex curiata* confirming the bestowal of *imperium* upon the consul Appius Claudius Pulcher was vetoed by the tribunes. He declared that he would go to his province without it; 'a consul ought to have a curiate law passed for him, but it was not necessary. Since he held his province by decree of the Senate, he would hold authority by the *Lex Cornelia* until he returned to the city'.[3] Cicero believed that such an act was unconstitutional, and wondered whether Lentulus would be justified in handing the province over to him. It is possible that Appius did not put his threat into action, and that he received a *lex curiata* after all.[4] He certainly made an attempt to obtain a faked law; what happened after this had been exposed is uncertain. On his return he demanded a triumph, which would have been an insult to the Senate if no *lex curiata* had been passed for him, and this were really indispensable. This may have been the very reason why he was later charged with treason by Dolabella. It is significant that in 54 he supported Pomptinus, whose request for a

[1] *Römisches Staatsrecht*, I, 54 (and note).
[2] *de leg. agr.* II, 11, 26ff.          [3] *ad fam.* I, 9, 25.
[4] So Tyrrell (*The Correspondence of Cicero*, II, 80) and Godt, in opposition to Lange: Mommsen is non-committal (*op. cit.* I, 55 n.).

triumph was blocked by Cato and Servilius on the ground
that he had gone to the province without a curiate law.
Cicero admits that one had been passed, but it had been
invalidated by some irregularity.[1] In view of Appius'
record in public and provincial life we may well believe
that he did not stand upon ceremony, and that he actually
left for Cilicia without having his authority confirmed in
the Curia; but there is little doubt that such an act was
highly unconstitutional if not positively illegal.

The installation of the new governor might present
some difficulties. In theory a governor should have
taken up his new duties on the day he retired from his
urban magistracy, but the formalities necessary before
his departure from Rome, and the slowness of transport,
usually made this impossible. Hence the function of the
new governor was suspended until he had taken over
from his predecessor. Before doing so he could only
fulfil those duties which belonged to his office in general,
or which were entrusted to him by a special decree of
the Senate. Thus Murena held a special levy in Umbria
on his way to Gaul as propraetor. It was considered a
rare privilege when Pompey took over the command of
Spain while remaining in Italy. In general the rule ran
that government, as apart from office, ran from the day
of entry into the province.[2]

Similarly, as soon as his successor arrived the old
governor's function lapsed; but Arnold is incorrect in
saying that he again became a private citizen. Again we
must distinguish between function and office, for Sulla
expressly allowed the pro-magistrate to retain his *im-*

[1] *ad Att.* IV, 18, 4 (IV, 16, 12).
[2] For a precise discussion of this point, see Mommsen, *op. cit.* II, 187.

*perium* until his return to the city.[1] This was to enable
the retiring proconsul to receive a triumph; Cicero
clung to his *imperium* throughout the early years of the
Civil War in desperate hopes of receiving such a reward. In more settled times some limits were placed
on the practice, for the *imperium* was abrogated by any
deliberate delay on the journey home. Quintus Cicero,
returning from Asia, called on his brother at Thessa-
lonica, but was unable to stay long with him in his
anxiety not to lose his *imperium*.[2]

An obvious danger was that the old governor might
be unwilling to hand over his command. Sulla definitely
ordained that the governor must leave his province
within thirty days of the arrival of his successor. Yet
even this allowed scope for conflicts of authority. There
was nothing to prevent a new governor from changing
his predecessor's arrangements. Pompey annulled the
dispositions of Lucullus, while Verres reversed a
judicial decision of his predecessor. In theory the old
governor was powerless to intervene, but he sometimes
attempted to assert his authority. We can sympathise
with Lucullus' resentment against Pompey's arbitrary
assumption of his command, if not with Appius' complaints against the beneficial reforms instituted by
Cicero. Gabinius refused to receive his successor, a
legate sent by Crassus, and held on to his command 'as
if it were immortal' until the arrival of Crassus himself.[3]

Rarely, however, did the retiring governor exercise
his dormant power save in matters of petty administration. Appius' conduct in holding assizes at Tarsus after

---

[1] *ad fam.* I, 9, 25.          [2] *ad Att.* III, 9, 1.
[3] Plut. *Luc.* 36; *II in Verr.* II, 28, 68; *ad Att.* VI, 1, 2; Dio xxxix, 60.

he knew of the arrival of Cicero was an insult which a less complaisant successor might well have resented. Cicero reminds him that a scrupulous governor even winds up his administrative duties some time before his successor's arrival to avoid any occasion for conflict. Appius also showed his contempt for the *novus homo* by deliberately avoiding a meeting with him, and Cicero came near to losing his dignity in following him round Cilicia. Usually however the change-over took place much more harmoniously.

A governor's term of office was automatically prorogued until the arrival of his successor, but he might wish to leave his province before this. He could not relinquish his duties before a successor had been appointed, but it does not seem that he was bound to await his arrival. Dio states that Caesar left Spain in 60 before his successor reached the country.[1] More orthodox governors, too, when their legal term of office was up, often left their provinces in the hands of a senior officer, usually a quaestor, but sometimes a legate. This was an extension of the old constitutional practice that a governor could grant his quaestor the powers of a propraetor during his absence on a lengthy expedition.[2] Cicero handed over the government of Cilicia to his young and inexperienced quaestor, C. Caelius Caldus, as soon as he heard of the appointment of his successor. He advised Q. Minucius Thermus, propraetor of Asia, to leave his quaestor C. Antonius in charge rather than a legate.[3] Bibulus on the other hand chose to entrust

[1] Dio, xxxvii, 54.

[2] Cf. Sall. *Jug.* 103: *consul in expeditionem proficiscens* (*Sullam*) *pro praetore reliquerat.*      [3] *ad fam.* ii, 18, 2.

his province to his legate Veiento. The practice was encouraged in later years by the partial disorganisation of the senatorial administration. We gather from Cicero that in 50 Cilicia, Syria, Africa, Macedonia, Bithynia and Asia were all left in the hands of either quaestors or legates.

Similarly the quaestor automatically took over the province on the death of the governor. In 43 P. Cornelius Lentulus took over Asia after Trebonius had been killed in battle; he styled himself *pro quaestore pro praetore* in writing to the Senate.[1] When Crassus was slain his quaestor Cassius took command of the broken army and defended Syria; with such success that he was left unrelieved for almost two years.

## REFORM OF THE SULLAN SYSTEM

It was only in the closing years of the republic that the Sullan system of appointing to provincial commands was radically altered. The details of this reform are still subject to controversy; there were four measures concerned, belonging to consecutive years:

54 B.C. Domitius Ahenobarbus and A. Claudius as consuls attempted to carry a decree of the Senate about the provincial commands, but this apparently fell through.[2]

53 B.C. Cn. Domitius and Valerius Messalla, the consuls, succeeded in passing a decree which probably had the same aim as that of the previous year. It enacted that no consul or praetor should take up a provincial command until five years after his period of office at Rome.[3]

---

[1] *ad fam.* XII, 15.    [2] *ad Att.* IV, 16, 5.
[3] Dio, XL, 46, 2.

52 B.C. Pompey as sole consul confirmed this decree with certain additions. The right of veto on the decrees of the Senate concerning consular provinces was restored to the Tribunes; and a special decree of the Senate was to decide the length of service in each province.[1]

51 B.C. M. Claudius Marcellus (consul) passed a law which is often referred to by Cicero;[2] the exact import of this is doubtful.

The controversy centres about the legislation of the year 52. Drumann and Mommsen[3] maintain that it was a mere decree of the Senate, confirmed by the law of Marcellus in the following year. Godt and Zumpt hold that it was included in Pompey's *Leges de iuribus magistratuum*, while Hofmann, Lange and Marquardt think that it was a separate law. This is most probable; for while the change of principle went so deep that a mere senatorial decree would have been inadequate, it seems fairly certain that the substantive measure was Pompey's. In this case, what was Marcellus' law of the following year? Drumann and Hofmann regard it as an ordinary *lex curiata de imperio* confirming the *imperium* of the governors; this is opposed by Mommsen and Godt. The latter suggests that it consisted of a *lex* and a *senatus consultum* introduced together in almost identical terms, and providing for the appointment of governors during the first five years of the new system. But it is difficult to suppose that Pompey would have overlooked such an important point, and there is a more possible explanation. The new governors would have lost their *imperium* by retirement into civil life. When

[1] Dio, XL, 56, 1.     [2] E.g. *ad fam.* XV, 9, 2; 14, 5.
[3] Drumann-Groebe, *Geschichte Roms.* III, 324; Mommsen, *op. cit.* II, 219.

there was no break between urban and provincial magistracy their authority went right on, and as we have seen even a *lex curiata may* have been unnecessary. To restore the lapsed *imperium* however was not so easy; Pompey may have enacted that it should be done by a *lex de imperio* brought before the *comitia tributa* or *centuriata* by the consuls of the year. Hence it was to Marcellus that Cicero owed his *imperium*. This would explain his gratitude to Marcellus and his assumption that he was personally interested in the length of his proconsulship. Corroborative evidence for this theory is supplied by Caesar's comment on the provincial appointments of the year 49: *Neque expectant praetores quod superioribus annis acciderat, ut de eorum imperio ad populum feratur*.[1]

More important than the circumstances of this reform are its cause and its effect. Lange thinks that its aim was to check the expenditure of candidates for office; if they had to wait five years for the chance of recouping themselves from a province, they would not be willing to pay so much for election. Hence too it would benefit the provincials, who would not have to contribute so much towards paying off the debts of the governor. Mommsen uncharitably points to the fact that for the next five years it would leave provincial appointments pretty well in the hands of the men in power, that is, Pompey and his friends. This is indeed one of the complaints put forward by Caesar,[2] but in reality the reform goes much deeper. By it the governorship first became a completely independent office. It was recognised that provincial government was no longer an appendage to

[1] *bell. civ.* 1, 6.    [2] *Ibid.* 1, 85.

an urban magistracy, but an equally important public service; in this sense the reform was a logical development of the Sullan system.

One important result of the reform is obvious. There would henceforth be no reason why a governor should not arrive in his province by the day on which his command legally began; a command could for the first time be given a fixed calendar reckoning. This was to have deep repercussions on Caesar's position in Gaul, as he could now be relieved on the very day—whichever it really was—on which his command terminated.[1]

Meanwhile, however, the new regulations could only come into force on their negative side. Some means had to be adopted to tide over the next few years until the magistrates for 52 were eligible for office. There were a number of ex-magistrates available who had never taken a province. These were now called on in turn, but it

---

[1] For a discussion of this question see articles by Stone (*Cl. Quart.* 1928, pp. 193–201) and Adcock (*ibid.* 1932, p. 14). The former favours the view that the command terminated on March 1, 50, the latter, with more plausibility, inclines towards the Ides of November of the same year. Professor Adcock's arguments may be summarised as follows: (*a*) The Gauls believed that Caesar's command legally terminated shortly after the summer of 50 (Hirtius, *B.G.* VIII, 39); (*b*) The Senate considered itself free to appoint a successor to Caesar in January of 49; (*c*) Caesar does not complain that the Senate has shortened the command allotted to him by the *Lex Pompeia Licinia*; (*d*) Appian and Dio agree in implying that Caesar's command terminated in 50; (*e*) Crassus left for his province on the Ides of November, 55. It is reasonable to suppose that his period of command coincided with the second quinquennium awarded to Caesar. There is no reason why the latter's second command should not overlap his first. Admittedly, the Ides is not a *dies comitialis*, but the command could be post-dated from the passing of the necessary *lex*; (*f*) Finally, the Ides of November played an important part in the controversy of the year (*ad fam.* VIII, 11, 3).

seems that a different procedure was adopted for 'consular' and 'praetorian' provinces. For the latter the five-year rule was given retrospective force; that is, in the year 53 the praetors of 58 would first be called on as far as they had not held provinces, and the remaining vacancies would be filled up from the whole order of ex-praetors in order of seniority. These emergency appointments were to be limited to one year, and fresh appointments were to be made annually in similar fashion. For example, in 50, when nine praetorian governors were wanted to fill the vacancies caused by the retirement of Cicero[1] and eight ex-praetors, the choice was first made from the praetorian college of 55.[2] Cato, who was praetor in 54, cast lots for a province in 49.

The consular provinces on the other hand seem to have been balloted for from the whole body of ex-consuls who had not taken a province, without regard for seniority. Thus the consular provinces for 51, Cilicia and Syria, fell to Cicero (consul 63) and Bibulus (59). Zumpt strangely maintains that the consular provinces were assigned to the senior available ex-consuls; but in this case we should have to explain why Aemilius Lepidus (66), Aurelius Cotta (65), and L. Caesar (64) were passed over. Nor can we accept his statement that a five-year interval was essential, as it was for the praetors. Caesar notes without comment that the two consular provinces for 49, Syria and Gaul,

[1] Cilicia had been made a praetorian province from party motives, to enable one of Caesar's provinces of Gaul to be transferred to another ex-consul.

[2] *ad fam.* VIII, 8, 8.

were allotted to Scipio (consul 52) and L. Domitius (consul 54) respectively.[1]

The new system never had a chance to show its positive merits; but it would probably have done much to raise the status of the governor and to benefit the provincials. If, as is likely, it was substantially due to Pompey, it was one of the few statesmanlike measures the Senate owed to this democrat turned constitutionalist.

## EXTRAORDINARY COMMANDS

For long before the Sullan Restoration the ultimate supremacy of the People had been an axiom of the Roman constitution. In the appointment to foreign command, the authority of the Senate had rarely been challenged, but on at least two occasions the rights of the sovereign People had been signally asserted. In the Second Punic War, Scipio ('Africanus') overcame the reluctance of the Senate to carry the war into Africa by threatening it with an appeal to the People: and it was by a direct vote of the People that the command in Africa against Jugurtha was transferred to Marius.

Even after Sulla had confirmed the authority of the Senate, the usual method of provincial appointment was often broken by means of extraordinary commands, for the common-sense of the Romans refused to be bound by the strict letter of the law. But these commands were not in themselves an attack on the constitution, and so

---

[1] *bell. civ.* I, 6. Caesar is careful to mention the fact that two eligible but unwilling ex-consuls, Philippus and Cotta (consuls 56 and 65), were deliberately omitted from the lot. If the five-year rule held, he would almost certainly have noted Scipio's appointment as illegal.

long as they were made and controlled by the Senate they served a useful and practical purpose. It was when the popular leaders, working through the *comitia*, obtained such grants of power for their own ends that the institution became dangerous. The commands of the decade 80–70 were pernicious only as establishing a precedent; judged on their own merits they could, and did, receive the support of the most faithful constitutionalist.

The first of these special commissions was granted under the aegis of Sulla himself, for from 82 to 79 the young Pompey enjoyed a special *imperium*, awarded through the Senate, in Sicily and Africa. This command gave a significant glimpse of Pompey's character; in his importunate demand for a triumph was to be seen that petty ambition which was to be so dangerous both to himself and to the Senate.

In 77 the rising of Lepidus gave him a fresh opportunity to show his undoubted military ability. Catulus was not a brilliant general and Pompey was commissioned to co-operate with him. Perhaps he was technically the legate of Catulus, but since Plutarch styles him στρα-τεύματος ἡγεμών he was more probably granted the rank of propraetor; even so he would still be Catulus' subordinate in theory.

On the suppression of Lepidus Pompey refused to disband his army, and demanded to be sent to Spain against Sertorius. This was granted at the motion of Philippus, despite some opposition, and he was despatched with proconsular *imperium*; his successes were a justification of the appointment from the practical point of view. It is difficult to agree with the strictures passed upon this command by those who judge it in the light of after-events. Arnold[1] states that the Senate 'practically nullified the policy of Sulla and stultified themselves'. Last[2] contents himself with styling it 'a fatal blow to the Sullan constitution'. But the Senate could not be expected to foresee the dangerous use Pompey would make of his privileges, and the eagerness with which the demagogues would turn this instrument to their own service. There was no other good general available. The measure was proposed in the Senate by a die-hard 'Tory'. The command, too, was only offered to Pompey after both the consuls had wisely refused it on the grounds of inexperience.[3] The command was not in itself entirely unconstitutional. One ex-consul, Metellus Pius, was already in Spain, and Pompey was to co-operate with him on equal terms.[4] Perhaps, as Boak suggests, he was formally granted *imperium pro consule* as governor of Hither Spain, for we do not know of any other governor being sent out after the death of Domitius. Nor must it be forgotten that strictly speaking Scipio Africanus Major had been just as unqualified when he took over the command in Spain.

The outbreak of the Third Mithridatic War in 74 called for vigorous action; the special command given to Lucullus was fraught with such importance that it deserves more detailed treatment.[5] In the same year extraordinary powers against the pirates were granted

[1] *Op. cit.* p. 51.

[2] *C.A.H.* ix, 318; but he is not insensible to the difficult problem before the Senate (*ibid.*).

[3] Cf. Philippus' quip that he was sent out *non pro consule sed pro consulibus* (*Phil.* xi, 8, 18).

[4] Val. Max. viii, 15: *pari imperio.*          [5] *V. infra*, chap. iv.

to the praetor Antonius by decree of the Senate. According to Asconius his province was to cover *tota ora
maritima*, and this is confirmed by the scholiast on
Juvenal.[1] The incompetence of Antonius led to his failure.
His command is significant mainly because Cicero refers
to it as *infinitum*.[2] This is the first time we hear of such
power. The 'Mediterranean Coast' furnished a very
loose boundary for his activities and in practice he could
enter into any of the coastal provinces and exert his
power there at will. As praetor, however, he would
always be subordinate to any governor with pro-
consular *imperium*.

In 72 the Senate granted *imperium extra ordinem* to
the consuls during the Servile War, but their failure
revealed the fact that more drastic measures were
necessary. Accordingly the praetor Crassus was appointed, not to co-operate with the consuls, but to
supersede them in the field.[3] He raised six new legions
by calling for volunteers and met with much success. At
the very close of the war he had the mortification of
seeing his rival Pompey associated with him. It had
been suggested that the Senate was in this case compelled to acquiesce in a vote of the Assembly, but it is
more probable, as Ferrero[4] thinks, that this appointment
too was directly due to the Senate.[5] It was the obvious step
to make doubly sure of the victory by sending the returned

[1] Asc. *in Verr.* I, 60, p. 176; Schol. *ad Juv.* VIII, 105. Cf. the appointment
of Sex. Pompeius to the *praefectura orae maritimae* in 39.

[2] *II in Verr.* II, 3, 8.

[3] Orosius (v, 24) asserts that this appointment was due to the Senate.

[4] *Op. cit.* (Eng. trans.), I, 173.

[5] Appian (*b.c.* I, 119) is vague: 'Those in the city...commissioned
Pompey.'

general to help Crassus. Purely practical too was the special command given to Metellus in Crete in 68, which was to lead to such a conflict of authority with Pompey.[1]

Hitherto all the special commands have been given by the Senate, and their holders have gone forth as its lieutenants. In the next decade the *comitia* was to be prodded into activity by the popular leaders and was to reassert its claims to make similar appointments. The Gabinian and Manilian Laws were not without precedent, but in their vast scope they marked a further step towards military monarchy. They had an important bearing on the position of Lucullus and will be discussed in detail in connection with him. Here it will be enough to consider their repercussions at Rome. The example of these two years showed what could be done by an ambitious general who could suborn a tribune to work for him. Caesar was not the man to miss his opportunity; and in 66/5 we find him angling unsuccessfully for a special command in Egypt.[2] The agrarian legislation of Rullus was another attempt to create an extraordinary command, but it was remarkable in that it proposed to put these powers into commission. It sought to establish an oligarchy of ten to counterbalance the military prestige of Pompey. The commissioners were to be elected for five years by a minority of the Tribes. Their province was to be the whole empire and their powers were almost unlimited. Cicero saw the dangers of such a scheme, particularly when a Caesar stood behind it, and his eloquence led to the withdrawal of the bill.

[1] Phlegon (*Frag. Hist. Graec.* III, 606) says that Metellus was sent to Crete with three legions.    [2] Suet. *Jul.* 11; *v. supra*, p. 67.

The last ten years of the Republic were to see these commands become even more far-reaching. In 59 Caesar as consul at last got the military command which he had coveted. The tribune Vatinius proposed a law by which he was to have the provinces of Cisalpine Gaul and Illyricum for five years, with three legions and the right to name his own legati, who were to be granted *imperium pro praetore*.[1] As is shown by the supplications subsequently passed in his honour, he was to be formally freed from that section of the *Lex Julia* which forbade expeditions out of the province. He was also to have the right of founding colonies at discretion; this right was later impugned in the controversy which arose over the urban magistrate of Novum Comum.

The bill was facilitated by means of a timely display of armed force arranged by Pompey. Meanwhile Transalpine Gaul had become vacant through the death of Metellus Celer, the governor-designate; and Pompey proposed in the Senate that it should be added to Caesar's command. A *senatus consultum* was passed to this effect, and the Senate at the same time increased Caesar's army by another legion. Many attempts have been made to explain this step away. It was alternatively a thin device to maintain prestige by stealing the popular party's thunder, or a *pis aller* to which they were driven in the absence of another possible candidate. Meyer suggests that the 'conservative' bloc in the Senate kept away from the house through fear, and that the decree was passed by the small Caesarian minority. Marsh thinks that the Senate wished to forestall an extension of the Vatinian

[1] The number of his legates is unknown, but in 58 there were at least six, and in 57 two more (Godt, *Quomodo provinciae...* p. 12).

Law by giving him the new province, but on a strictly *annual* tenure. Cary[1] goes so far as to suggest that the Senate deliberately sent Caesar out to a difficult post in the hope that he might fail; but even if Ariovistus' boast that the death of Caesar would be welcomed at Rome was not entirely unfounded, it is no justification for this hypothesis. The Senate had too deep a fear of a Gallic invasion to risk the security of the frontier for the sake of a petty personal triumph, and its decision was due entirely to practical motives. The *Lex Vatinia* and the death of Metellus had completely altered the situation since Caesar had originally been fobbed off with a minor province. In any case there were no fixed parties in the Senate, and in matters where the opinion of the house was fairly evenly divided it could reverse its previous decision with all the facility of a continental chamber of deputies.

The consuls of 58, the infamous Gabinius and Piso, were rewarded for their support of Clodius by the grant of extraordinary powers. At first it was arranged that Piso should go to Macedonia and Gabinius to Cilicia, but the latter's province was changed to Syria. Macedonia and Cilicia may have been already assigned as the consular provinces for the year; the irregularity lay rather in the special powers given to the consuls, the extended bounds of their provinces, and the manner in which they were appointed. They received their *imperium* through the *comitia* without consulting the Senate. To each of them a province was assigned by name without the use of the lot. Mommsen thinks that the provinces were not named in the law, but this is

[1] Meyer, *op. cit.* p. 93; Marsh, *op. cit.* p. 106; Cary, *C.A.H.* IX, 519.

definitely stated by Cicero.[1] Piso received rights of jurisdiction over the free peoples of Achaia, Thessaly, Athens and Greece in general, in contravention of the *Leges Juliae*. Cicero's references to *imperium infinitum* must however be discounted as rhetoric. Mommsen suggests that the law may have authorised Gabinius' expedition to Egypt, but from Cicero's condemnation of him[2] it seems more likely that it did not expressly allow him to conduct foreign wars on his own responsibility. Both generals received an unusually generous *ornatio*; perhaps too they were granted the right to enlist troops at pleasure. The number of their legates is unknown, but it was apparently exceeded by Piso. It is certain that he chose them himself, and made appointments which were unwelcome to the Senate.[3]

The consuls set out from Rome before the end of the year 58. The tenure of their command was not fixed, but the Senate saw to it that they were relieved as soon as possible. The attempt to appoint successors for 56 was blocked, but both provinces were named as 'praetorian' for the following year.

The year 57 saw another command created for Pompey. A sudden shortage of corn led Cicero to suggest that he be appointed superintendent of the corn supply for five years. He was granted full powers to purchase corn and hire transport, and received pro-consular *imperium* (*imperium infinitum aequum*). He was allowed to nominate up to fifteen legates; and with un-usual grace he offered Cicero the first post. This was a straightforward and practical command. More interest-

---

[1] *de dom.* 9, 23: *nominatim.*        [2] *pro Rab. Post.* 8, 19 ff.
[3] *pro Sest.* 14, 33.

ing is the rival proposal put forward by the tribune
Messius, by which Pompey was to have *imperium maius*,
that is, supreme over-riding powers over all other
governors. As Cicero remarks,[1] his own motion was
modest in comparison. It was rightly rejected by the
Senate as being unnecessarily sweeping in its scope.
Probably Pompey was sincere in preferring to accept
the lesser command, which would give him all the power
he needed, together with a position in which he might
indulge his vanity. As Meyer maintains, Pompey
merely desired to be the first man in the State and never
aspired to absolute monarchy.

It was agreed at the Conference of Lucca that all three
Triumvirs should receive special commands. In 56
Pompey and Crassus carried a consular law prolonging
Caesar's term in Gaul, while a friendly tribune Trebonius proposed in the *comitia* that Pompey should receive both Spains, and Crassus Syria, for five years. The
Senate had named Syria and Macedonia as consular
provinces; but a recurrence of trouble in Spain readily
induced them to agree to the supersession of Metellus
Nepos, the weak governor of Nearer Spain,[2] and the
union of the two provinces under one strong man. But
it could not be expected calmly to acquiesce in the unprecedented powers granted by the law, and Cato was
not the only senator to oppose the bill with all his power.
Nor did the partisans of Caesar conceal their mistrust;
but the measure was eventually carried and the consuls
took over their commands immediately. Perhaps they
cast lots or came to some agreement about their re-
spective provinces, but more probably these were

[1] *ad Att.* IV, 1, 7.   [2] Dio, XXXIX, 44.

directly named in the law. Each governor was to have a large army. Plutarch gives Pompey four legions, but it rather appears that he actually had six,[1] and he was granted power to enlist troops at will; Crassus crossed the Euphrates with seven legions.

A. The exact scope of the governors has caused controversy. By a special dispensation they were allowed the right of making war and peace on their own responsibility. For this reason some of our authorities say that 'Libya and Spain' were given to Pompey, some 'Syria and Egypt' to Crassus, or even that he was directly entrusted with the conduct of a Parthian War;[2] but all these suppositions can be disproved. We know that Africa and Cyrenaica were under independent governors in the following years;[3] hence Pompey can at most have had permission to wage war in Mauretania if necessary. Egypt was not included in Crassus' province, for the Piper had been restored by Gabinius that very year. Nor can a 'Parthian War' have been expressly included in his commission. Apart from Plutarch's evidence[4] it would have been an unnecessary addition in view of his general exemption from the *Lex Julia*.[5] There seems no doubt that the actual provinces of the pair were Syria and the two Spains respectively.

B. These commands provided a further development in the system of government by deputy. Crassus sent a legate on ahead to take over the command from

---

[1] Godt, *op. cit.* p. 25.     [2] Livy, *Ep.* 105.

[3] Caesar, *bell. civ.* I, 31; *ad fam.* VIII, 8, 8.

[4] Plutarch, *Crass.* 16.

[5] I.e. the *Lex Julia de repetundis* (59 B.C.), which confirmed the *Lex Cornelia de maiestate* by forbidding a governor to wage war on his own responsibility (*v. infra*, p. 158).

Gabinius. Pompey never went near his province at all. His duties in connection with the corn-supply kept him in Rome, and he found that he could manage the affairs of a difficult province quite well by means of trusted subordinates. In fact, the two Spains stood to Pompey in exactly the same relation as the imperial provinces were to stand to the emperor.

The *Lex Trebonia* promulgated the last of the great provincial commands of the Republic. From the long series which gradually led up to the autocracy of Caesar, certain principles of general application can be drawn:

A. The commands could be 'extraordinary' in three ways: either the scope of the command, the qualifications of the holder, or the method of appointment. Until 70 the Senate appointed to command, but sometimes its nominees were unqualified and sometimes the province was enlarged. Later the method of appointment, through the *comitia*, became equally irregular. At the end of the period these commands, instituted for practical ends, became more and more the prize of ambitious generals; and the command was created for the man rather than the man for the command.

B. The Senate did not however completely lose its hold on these commands. Most of them had some practical justification. The Senate usually confirmed, or even increased the scope of, the powers granted by the *comitia*. The commands of Gabinius and Piso are the only instances where the Senate apparently failed to prevent the appointment of two incapable wastrels as a result of arrant jobbery. And even here we must beware of too wholesale a condemnation. Their misdeeds may well have been grossly exaggerated by Cicero. Meyer has shown that it is possible to take a more favourable view of Gabinius' proconsulship at least.[1]

C. At first these commands, like the usual provincial commands, were unlimited in tenure. Consequently their holder could be recalled at the will of the Senate. As they became wider in scope, a definite time-limit was applied to them. This apparent limitation was more important as a minimum than as a maximum, for it meant that the governor could not be superseded for a fixed number of years. Hence the *comitia* could recall Lucullus from Asia; but it could not have superseded Pompey in Spain in 53 without a deep breach of the constitution. It was this point which eventually enabled Caesar to enter Italy as the defender of Roman law and constitutional principle.[2]

[1] Meyer, *op. cit.* p. 166.

[2] When the consul Marcellus proposed in 51 to terminate Caesar's command, his colleague Sulpicius, the jurist, upheld the principle that a governor who had committed no crime could not be deposed from his command until his legal term had expired (*C.A.H.* IX, 629). Marcellus could of course justify his attempt to revoke the *Lex Licinia Pompeia* by citing the principle *salus populi suprema lex.*

## CHAPTER IV

## LUCULLUS AND POMPEY

$W_E$ are now in a position to discuss the extraordinary command held by Lucullus in Asia. This is significant not only in itself, but in the personality of its protagonist; for in L. Licinius Lucullus we may see the fine flower of the Sullan Restoration. He was a lieutenant of Sulla whose life extended almost to the close of the period. His political career brings us into contact with all the most important crises. His extraordinary command against Mithridates foreshadowed the military monarchy of the future. His recall in 66 was the culminating triumph of the Equites. As consul at Rome, as governor of Asia, and as commander of the East, he had to settle administrative and military problems which were of vital importance. Above all, he united extraordinary talent with an unusual loyalty towards the letter and the spirit of the Sullan constitution. Historians, preoccupied with the more popular statesmen of the day, and naturally unsympathetic towards the unsuccessful man, have strangely neglected this figure, whose career ended in such a disappointing fashion;[1] yet Lucullus, above all others, illustrates by his life and his character the strength and weakness of the Sullan system.

[1] The most detailed authority for the life of Lucullus is Gelzer's monumental article in Pauly-Wissowa's *Realencyclopädie* (vol. XIII, 1; Licinius (Lucullus) no. 104). Of the historians, Ferrero alone gives him due attention (*The Greatness and Decline of Rome*, vol. I).

Lucullus was sprung from one of the most honourable of the plebeian clans, the *gens Licinia*, while through his mother he was connected with the great family of the Metelli. He was born not later than 117. Together with his brother Marcus he received an excellent education; and when he was only eighteen he appeared in the law-courts as the prosecutor of Gaius Servilius, who had been the instrument of his father's exile two years previously.

On the outbreak of the Social War in 90 Lucullus secured an appointment as military tribune, and showed himself a bold yet cautious officer. He was allotted to Sulla as quaestor for 87, and his talent very quickly attracted the attention of the great general. It was Lucullus who was sent ahead to Greece to take over the command against Mithridates in Sulla's name. He too was entrusted with the responsible task of collecting a fleet from Egypt and Syria. It was while he was sailing along the coast of Lydia to rejoin Sulla that Fimbria, the Marian commander, sought his co-operation. His refusal to accept Fimbria's overtures may have meant a new lease of life for Mithridates, but no other course was possible for a man of his stamp. If he had acceded to Fimbria's request he would have been guilty of the grossest personal and party disloyalty. He would have betrayed his own general—for there could never be aught but war between Sulla and the Marians whom Fimbria represented—and he would have betrayed the deepest principles of his life. He was an aristocrat born and bred. 'Among the many adventurers who took part in the struggles of this decade he was one of those few young nobles who consistently fought for the pure aristocratic tradition of the old times.' Drumann condemns his answer as a 'mere party move', but it was something higher than that.[1]

After the conclusion of the Peace of Dardanus the onerous duty of collecting the vast war indemnity from the province of Asia was committed to Lucullus. He performed his office with justice and humanity. It is true that honorific inscriptions cannot always be taken at their face value, but the number of such testimonials which has been found does seem to indicate that Lucullus tried to lighten the burden by fair and equitable dealing.[2] Unfortunately he was unable to prevent the communities from adopting the speciously attractive course of borrowing the money from Roman capitalists—at exorbitant rates of interest. His personal observation must have impressed him with the evils of such a system; and he was left with a rooted distrust of the *negotiatores*, and a determination to clip their wings as soon as he had the power to do so.

When Sulla returned to Rome in 84 Lucullus remained in Asia to serve as proquaestor to the governor L. Licinius Murena. He refrained from supporting the unprovoked attack which his feckless superior made on Mithridates, and spent his time in pacifying the coastal districts. But after seven years in the East he was naturally eager to return home to continue his official career; and after initiating an expedition against Mity-

[1] *Op. cit.* p. 137.

[2] For example, Synnada honours him as 'patron and benefactor' (*I.G.R.* IV, 701), Thyatira as 'saviour, benefactor, and constitutional reformer' because of his uprightness and goodwill towards the city (*I.G.R.* IV, 1191); an inscription at Delos in his honour probably dates from the same period (Dessau, 865).

lene, he handed the siege over to Murena's successor, the propraetor Minucius Thermus, and left for Rome.

Sulla had not forgotten his faithful lieutenant. The dictator used his influence at the elections, and Lucullus landed in Italy in 80 to find that he had already been elected aedile, with his brother, for the following year. Such election in absence was not unprecedented, but it was an unusual honour.[1] It will be remembered that the Senate deliberately refused Caesar's request for a similar privilege in 60.

Lucullus' year of office was eventful only for the magnificent games given by him and his brother; but he must have given convincing proof of his powers of administration, for during his very year of office he was elected praetor for the next year (78).[2] Such an election was unorthodox, but perhaps he received a special dispensation from the *Lex annalis* which governed the *cursus honorum*. It is probable that Sulla, now living in retirement, again used his influence on Lucullus' behalf. The dictator had always had an especial sympathy for his loyal quaestor, who did not pester him for rewards and extraordinary commands. His death, which occurred in 78, showed the high place Lucullus held in his affections. He paid a graceful compliment to his literary interests by dedicating his memoirs to him, and requesting that he would edit them before publication; while in his will he asked Lucullus to act as guardian to his infant son Faustus. Pompey, the rising star of Rome,

---

[1] Previous instances of such election in absence were the elections of Marius as consul in 104 and 101, and C. Cornelius Cethegus as curule aedile in 199.

[2] *Acad. pr.* ii, 1, 1: *continuo praetor.*

was not even mentioned in the testament; this deliberate
omission stung Pompey to the quick, and sowed the
seeds of his lifelong rivalry with Lucullus.

The main political interest of the year 78 was the
quarrel between the two consuls Catulus and Lepidus;
but Lucullus had probably left for his province of Africa
before Lepidus broke into open rebellion. As propraetor in
Africa he upheld his reputation as a just and sympathetic governor. Groebe remarks that 'he did not remain
there above the normal time', but Cicero implies that he
certainly did not return to Rome before 75.[1] In that
year he was eligible to stand for the consulate. By now
his name and achievements were well known to the
electorate. He was supported by the best of the nobility, and had little difficulty in securing election with
M. Aurelius Cotta as his colleague.

## LUCULLUS AS CONSUL

Lucullus entered upon his year of office as consul at a
time of great difficulty, for both at home and abroad
there were problems which demanded wise and statesmanlike handling. His colleague was by birth and in-
clination a member of the 'moderate nobility' and was
not likely to repeat the rôle of Lepidus; but he had
neither the talent nor the principle of his brother and
predecessor, Gaius, and Lucullus soon saw that the
burden of decision would rest with him.

The first question Lucullus was called upon to deal
with concerned his rival Pompey. Since Pompey arrived
in Spain, both he and Metellus Pius had gained victories

[1] *Acad. pr.* II, 1, 1: . . .*post in Africam, inde ad consulatum.* . . .

in the open field. But now Sertorius had taken to guerilla warfare, a system which has always proved exasperatingly effective in the mountains of Spain. Pompey, worn out by shortage of supplies and the pin-pricks of the enemy, sent a long and peremptory despatch to the Senate during the year 75. In this he declared that unless fresh stores and reinforcements were sent out to him, he would have no other course than to return to Italy with his army. The thinly veiled threat was not lost on the Senate. If Pompey returned, with his army at his back, nobody at Rome would dare gainsay him. He would be able to impose his own con-ditions on the Senate, and his previous actions had not been such as to enable this prospect to be viewed with equanimity. Hence the majority of the Senate was will-ing to accede to Pompey's demands. Lucullus too in-clined towards the same view. It is usual to attribute his decision to purely personal motives; he was fright-ened of further provoking his brilliant young rival, and feared that his return might compromise that command in the East for which he was already hoping. These thoughts may have passed through his mind, but he was probably actuated by higher considerations. If Pompey carried out his threat, it seemed as if the Senate would either have to surrender tamely to him, or embark upon a civil war of very doubtful issue; for it was not as yet realised that Pompey need not be taken seriously as a leader of the revolution. Moreover, his demands were justified on practical grounds. Sertorius was still a dangerous enemy, and he could only be finally sup-pressed if the Roman generals had ample resources. If the Roman armies withdrew, his dream of leading a

Marian crusade against the capital might yet materialise. It was commonly said at Rome, that if Pompey left Spain, Sertorius would be in the city before him. Above all, Lucullus was a soldier himself and looked at the matter from the soldier's point of view. Whether the Senate had acted wisely or not in giving the Spanish command to Pompey, it was its duty to support him to the best of its ability. Hence it was that he sponsored Pompey's request when it came before the Senate at the beginning of the year, and secured authority to despatch the necessary men and supplies.

Meanwhile the constitutional issue had again been raised. Ever since the death of Sulla there had been a movement, instigated by the 'popular' leaders, to secure the restoration of the tribunate; this office, misused as it was, was still regarded as the keystone of the old democracy. In the previous year the consul C. Aurelius Cotta had made a well-meaning but misguided effort to broaden the constitution by restoring to the tribunes the right of standing for higher office. This was a dangerous concession, and one that ran directly counter to the whole intention of the Sullan reforms, but Cotta, who was one of the most loyal and respected members of the nobility, succeeded in persuading the Senate to agree to it for the sake of peace. He soon recognised his mistake. The measure failed in its aim, for the agitation still went on. The only result was that men of spirit and ambition were once more attracted into this office.

The two most troublesome tribunes in the year 74 were L. Quinctius and P. Cornelius Cethegus. The former was a glib-tongued demagogue whose object was to secure the complete abolition of all the checks which Sulla had imposed upon the tribunate; the latter was notorious as the most unscrupulous intrigant in Rome. Lucullus was afraid of neither. He made it clear in his speeches that he would not countenance any further constitutional reforms during his year of office; he also saw Quinctius privately and reminded him of the fate of Lepidus. He publicly rebuked Cethegus for his loose living, and advised him to take his official duties a little more seriously. By this means he earned the undying hatred of both magistrates; but they paid him the compliment of relapsing into uneasy silence until he left Rome for the East. His prompt and firm handling of the subversive elements in the State was an object-lesson which the Senate was strangely slow to apply. It showed that the agitation for constitutional reform was largely fostered by the demagogues and did not rest on any deep-seated popular movement; it showed too of what poor stuff most of the demagogues were made.

The chief interest of the year, however, centred round foreign affairs. Pompey's gloomy dispatch from Spain was followed by alarming rumours from the East. The northern barbarians were harassing Macedonia, and piracy had again become acute throughout the eastern Mediterranean. The pacification of Macedonia was finally achieved by the consul of the following year, Lucullus' brother, but the question of the pirates could no longer be postponed. Lucullus had seen their power and the harm they wrought at first hand, and it was with his support, if not at his suggestion, that the Senate decided to institute an extraordinary command to deal with them. Obviously local action was of little effect, and it was only by a concerted drive that the pests could be swept from the seas. The command was a very practical attempt to tackle a difficult problem. Despite the wide scope of the proposed *imperium*—the whole sea and the coastland up to a depth of fifty miles—it was in no way inconsonant with the letter or the spirit of the Sullan restoration. The commander was to be appointed by the Senate, and it would be as its servant that he held his office.

Unfortunately the success of the scheme was stultified by the appointment of a very mediocre figure to the command. Admittedly Rome had at this period few generals of the first rank available, but it should have been possible to find somebody better than M. Antonius 'Creticus', one of the praetors for the year. We are told that the appointment of such an inefficient commander was due especially to the intrigues of Cethegus; he was supported by the consul Cotta, who was probably a personal friend of Antony's. The Senate acquiesced because, after experiencing the presumption of Pompey, it feared to place a strong man in a post of such power. But by this excessive caution it ruined a well-planned campaign; and in postponing the suppression of the pirates it made itself directly responsible for the far more dangerous command which was given to Pompey in 67.

## THE COMMAND IN ASIA

Meanwhile the Eastern Question had once more come into the foreground. Late in the year 75 or early in 74 died Nicomedes III of Bithynia, and it was found in his will that he had bequeathed his kingdom to the Roman People. Such, at least, is the evidence of the over-

whelming majority of the ancient historians.[1] One
scholiast alone tells us that Nicomedes died intestate.[2]
It is true that a pretender soon arose who claimed to be
the legitimate son of the late monarch, but this was an
obvious, in fact inevitable, gambit in all cases of succession in the East. Even the indecent haste with which the
Bithynians tumbled over themselves to testify against
his claims cannot make us accept the suspicions of those
who would reject the will as forged or non-existent, and
the witnesses as suborned.[3] At all events, it was generally accepted as a genuine testament at Rome; the only
question was whether the bequest should be accepted or
not.

The Senate clearly realised that the annexation of
Bithynia would bring her into immediate contact with
that dangerous neighbour Mithridates, and would almost certainly lead to war with him; but its first instinct
to refuse the bequest was soon tempered by other
considerations.

In the first place, the war with Mithridates could at
best only be postponed and not avoided. Sooner or later
a collision was bound to occur, and it had better come
before the king had grown any stronger. Already he
had opened negotiations with Sertorius and the pirates.
It was at his instigation that his son-in-law Tigranes
had overrun Cappadocia. His agents were at work
rousing the Danubian tribes against Rome. He could
rely on the support of the Cilicians and he had secured

[1] Appian, *bell. civ.* I, 111; Eutrop. VI, 6; Vell. II, 4; Arrian, *fr.* 24;
Livy, *Ep.* 93; Ampelius, 33, 3.

[2] Schol. *Gronov.* p. 437, Orelli.

[3] Sall. *h.* II, 71: *Quos adversum multi ex Bithynia volentes accurrere
falsum filium argituri.*

the goodwill, if not the active co-operation, of the kings
of Egypt and Cyprus. If the Romans had relinquished
their claims to Bithynia he would have installed a puppet-
prince of his own on the throne; the annexation of the
country, and then the invasion of Asia, would only have
been a matter of time.

There was, moreover, another factor to be taken into
account. Whether or no, as Ferrero suggests,[1] Bithynia
was already permeated with Roman financiers, it is
certain that the capitalist class at Rome looked forward
to the incorporation of such a rich field of activity with
lively anticipation. The Senate could not afford to neglect
the interests of such a powerful class; and with both the
military and the financial motives in view, it came to the
momentous decision to accept the bequest. It is significant that a big 'chartered company' was immediately
formed by some of the leading Equites for the exploitation of the new province.

The first thing to do was to occupy Bithynia with a
strong force. Rome had four legions in Asia Minor; but
while the governor of Asia, M. Juncus, was hopelessly
incompetent, his colleague in Cilicia, Octavius, the
consul of 75, was either dying or already dead. It was
to Juncus that the Senate sent orders to take over the
province; but before he could move Mithridates had
taken action. He altruistically declared himself the
protector of the young pretender, and invaded Bithynia,
through Paphlagonia, on his behalf.

The Senate had already declared the new province
'consular' for the next year, together with Cisalpine
Gaul. Unfortunately the lot on this occasion behaved

[1]. *Op. cit.* I, 148.

in a most perverse manner, for it gave Bithynia to Aurelius Cotta, who was obviously unequal to the task before him. It was just the command for which Lucullus wished, for he was burning to cross swords with his old antagonist, but Cotta, like most weak men, was far too proud to resign his position to him. At this moment the news of the death of Octavius reached Rome, and provided Lucullus with fresh hope. Could he get himself transferred from Gaul to Cilicia? The Senate would surely want to send a strong governor to the vacant province, and it could effect the change without inconvenience.

Unfortunately Lucullus had roused considerable personal enmity by his activities as consul, and there were many who would oppose any such suggestion from petty spite. It was even possible that his rival Pompey would be recalled from Spain to take over the post. Many of the other nobles too were known to be scheming for it. Finally Lucullus decided to swallow his pride. Rather than lose the appointment he made advances to Praecia, the notorious courtesan and confidante of Cethegus. She soon became his firm ally, and through her he secured the good offices of his enemy the tribune. The influence of Cethegus had its effect, and Lucullus received the province of Cilicia by the unanimous vote of the Senate. At the same time it was recognised that the gravity and extent of the coming war demanded a greater coordination of action than was afforded by the ordinary system of provincial government. It was not enough to send Lucullus to Cilicia if Asia were to be left open to Mithridates. Accordingly it was decided that the incapable Juncus should be recalled to Rome and his

province too given to Lucullus. Finally the Senate
formally entrusted Lucullus with the conduct of the war
against Mithridates. This meant that while Cotta would
still hold the province of Bithynia he would be definitely
subordinate to his colleague in military matters, and
Lucullus would be able to lead troops into his province
if necessary without transgressing the strict laws of
provincial administration. As a sop to his pride, it was
also decreed that Cotta should have the comparatively
unimportant command of the Roman fleet.

There is no reason to doubt the substantial truth of
Plutarch's account of the way in which Lucullus got his
command. Admittedly it is not a pleasant episode in
his career. But to a Roman there would be nothing
morally wrong in such a transaction; and we must remember too that it is only a couple of generations since
boudoir diplomacy went out of fashion in modern Europe.
And if ever the end justified the means it was in this case.
Lucullus was pre-eminently the man for the job. Of the
only two Romans who could be compared with him as
generals, Metellus Pius and Pompey, the former was
an old man, while it would have been unsafe to have
withdrawn the latter from Spain as yet. His well-known
philhellenism made him an appropriate man to rally
the Greeks of Asia against the 'barbarian'. He had
himself served against Mithridates; and his personal
knowledge of the terrain was of especial importance in
the days when scientific charts and maps were unknown.
He knew, too, the conditions and feelings of the peoples
of Asia Minor. Above all, he was a perfectly 'safe' man
who was unlikely to presume upon his powers.

Two minor points are of interest in this command.

The one is that the two consuls left Rome well before their year of office was up. This was, however, as we have seen above, by no means unprecedented; and it was urgently necessary in view of the kaleidoscopic changes in the East. Secondly, the fact that Lucullus was formally entrusted with the conduct of the war makes his lengthy tenure of command quite constitutional; for he would naturally be expected to hold it until the war was finished.

There has been considerable disagreement both in ancient and in modern times about the exact scope of Lucullus' command. Willems suggests that he received only the province of Asia, other writers insist that he was appointed governor of Cilicia, and only later given authority in Asia.[1] But Velleius expressly states that he held the province of Asia immediately after his consulate.[2] His activity in Asia in the first years of the war proves that he had full authority there; and the fact that we know of no governor between M. Juncus and the propraetor of 68 seems to show that Lucullus held the office both *de iure* and *de facto*, from the very beginning of the war.

## LUCULLUS IN ASIA

It must have been the middle of summer, 74, when Lucullus and Cotta left for the East.[3] On landing in Asia, Lucullus found that Mithridates had already occu-

[1] Willems, *op. cit.* II, 581,[1] Ferrero, *op. cit.* (Eng. trans.), II, 537; Lange, *R.A.* III (2), 206; Marsh, *op. cit.* p. 70.

[2] Vell. II, 33, 1: *ex consulatu sortitus Asiam*; see Rice Holmes, *The Roman Republic*, I, 179.

[3] For a full discussion of this point, as of the chronology of the war in general, see Rice Holmes, *op. cit.* I, 398 ff.

pied almost the whole of Bithynia. Owing to the straitened financial situation at Rome, he had only been able
to bring one fresh legion with him. Hence his first task
was to collect and organise the very mixed body of
Roman troops already in the East. While the concentration of the legions was proceeding, he was able to
concern himself to some extent with the economic
conditions of the province of Asia. Finally, in the late
autumn of the same year, he marched his troops into the
hinterland on the first stage of their long campaigns.

The struggle against Mithridates falls conveniently
into two divisions. The first begins with the battle of
Chalcedon, culminates at Cabira, and ends with the fall
of the great fortresses of Heraclea and Amisus. Then,
after a winter spent in the administration of Asia,
Lucullus captured Sinope, the last stronghold of Mithridates, and began his advance against Tigranes. The
brilliant campaign of Tigranocerta proved the summit
of his success; rejected by his soldiers, and recalled by
the home government, he left it to another to reap the
fruit of his victories.

The strategy and tactics of Lucullus have been ex-
haustively discussed by Munro, Eckhardt and Rice
Holmes.[1] His high qualities as a general and an administrator are now generally admitted. He was the
real conqueror of Mithridates, for the king's reconquest
of Pontus was a mere flash in the pan. He led his legions
into lands no Roman eyes had ever seen. He enriched
himself and his soldiers without losing the affection of
the provincials, he conducted his campaigns at no cost
to the Treasury, and yet he scrupulously preserved the

[1] See Bibliography.

unwritten conventions of warfare. Above all, he performed these feats with a sullen and unenthusiastic army
beneath him, and a lukewarm government at his back.
His colleague Cotta was incompetent if not actively
disloyal; and crowned his ineptitude by ingloriously returning to Rome and leaving his command vacant. His
own lieutenant Clodius sedulously fostered sedition in
the camp. Lucullus could rely on nothing save his own
powers; and the fact that he came so near his aim shows
that his boundless confidence in himself was justified.

And yet Lucullus failed. The smouldering discontent
in his camp broke into open mutiny. His command in
Asia was steadily lessened by the home government,
and successors were appointed to relieve him in his
various provinces. He was compelled to look impotently
on while Mithridates and Tigranes recovered a large
part of their losses. At this inopportune moment (67)
arrived the 'Commission of Ten' which had been sent
out to organise the new provinces of Rome. Lucullus
can scarcely have welcomed such a pointed reminder of
the contrast between his former triumphs and his present
helplessness, but he received the commissioners with all
courtesy; and we find them in the following year co-
operating with him in some details of the organisation
of Pontus which were afterwards annulled by Pompey.

In the autumn of 67 the Fimbrian soldiers actually
carried out their intentions and left the camp of Lucullus
in disorderly enthusiasm; the rest of his troops Lucullus
formally handed over to a representative of Glabrio,
the new governor of Bithynia. He did not as yet return
to Rome, for he still retained his personal *imperium* and
his authority as president of the commission, and he

occupied himself during the winter of 67/6 in attending to the organisation of the new province of Pontus. The condition of Roman Asia during these months is well expressed by Reinach when he says that it contained 'two armies without generals, and a general without an army'.[1] But there was on the coast of Cilicia another general, a general with an army; and Pompey was only awaiting the authority to act, to recover the ground lost during the year 67.

## THE RECALL OF LUCULLUS

The downfall and recall of Lucullus deserves full discussion as marking the turning-point in the struggle between the Senate and its opponents for the control of foreign policy. It is usually attributed to three causes: the ambition of Pompey, the vindictive resentment of the Equites, and the mutiny of the army. But there is no doubt that the last factor was largely the result of the first two. The discontent of the army obviously provided a favourable ground for sedition-mongers, for the natural lawlessness of the soldiers was aggravated by Lucullus' lack of personal popularity. Yet it is extremely doubtful whether this discontent would ever have come to a head in open mutiny of its own accord. Sallust says that the soldiers were disaffected towards Lucullus from the very beginning of the war. If they had been going to revolt they could have done so earlier. Lucullus reduced the disorderly rabble of the Fimbrian legions into a disciplined army during his first two months

[1] *Mithridate Eupator*, p. 378. The phrase is borrowed from Caesar (Suetonius, *Div. Jul.* 34).

in Asia. Only once during the first six years of
the war—at the capture of Amisus—did the soldiers
break into open disobedience, and then discipline was
restored after the first madness of plunder had passed
away. It was these 'disaffected' soldiers that won for
Lucullus his greatest victories; until 68 they had probably never thought of mutiny, even when the discipline
of Lucullus was weighing most heavily on them.

The fact that many of them were due for discharge in
67 may have made the campaigns seem still more irksome, but this was a pretext rather than a cause for the
mutiny.[1] Until the end of the year this could scarcely
be put forward as a just grievance; and even then Lucullus would have been quite within his rights in postponing demobilisation until the war had been finished.
It is a striking fact that the majority of these 'war-
weary' veterans promptly re-enlisted for a further spell
of active service under Pompey!

There were two things which fanned the long-
smouldering embers of discontent into flame. The one
was the knowledge that Lucullus' position was being
steadily undermined by the home government, and that
he could now be defied with impunity. The other was
the activity of the agitators in the army. We can scarcely
doubt that Clodius and his fellows were acting at the
direct instigation of the 'anti-Lucullan' party at Rome.
It is significant that when Clodius found Lucullus' camp
too hot to hold him, he was received with open arms by

---

[1] The 'Fimbriani' had been enrolled at Rome in 86; and during the
first century B.C., twenty years' service was regarded as the normal
maximum for the legionary. The formal recall of these troops in 67
(v. infra, p. 122) seems to recognise this principle.

his brother-in-law Marcius Rex, the newly arrived governor of Cilicia, who promptly put him in charge of his fleet.

It was Pompey and the Equites, then, who were primarily responsible for the recall of Lucullus. Each of them had real or fancied grievances to inflame their ill-feeling against him. Pompey had been jealous of him ever since the marked omission of his own name from Sulla's testament. The rivalry between the two men was increased by the difference in their aims and ideals. Lucullus stood for the traditional supremacy of the Senate, and for the maintenance of the Sullan constitution, Pompey foreshadowed in his ideals and his career the military monarchy that was to take its place. Both men were sound administrators and good generals, but Pompey was a less rigid disciplinarian, and was more amenable to compromise. For this very reason he could place more reliance on his soldiers; he had, too, the faculty of exacting personal affection from his equals and his inferiors alike. The downfall of Lucullus, on the other hand, was facilitated by his strange inability to win the sympathy of those with whom he worked.

Pompey was ten years younger than Lucullus, but his precocious rise to power more than wiped out the difference in years. We have seen how his absence in Spain prevented him from competing with his elder for the command in the East, yet even this inflamed his jealousy. He was constitutionally incapable of regarding greatness in another without a feeling of personal grievance, even if his own position were not affected by it. Nor was his resentment lessened by the news of Lucullus' brilliant successes in Pontus.

After his consulship in 70 Pompey, the restless and ambitious general, surprised Rome by retiring into private life without taking a province. It is too much to expect that he merely sat in Olympian calm for three years until some occasion should arise for his services. The whole course of events seems to show that he had a deliberate aim in view in this manœuvre. He refused to take a province because he was already intriguing for the transference of Lucullus' command to himself. Such a supposition is quite in keeping with his character, and helps to explain the history of the next three years.

Lucullus, however, still had far too strong a body of supporters in the Senate to permit of such a bare-faced piece of jobbery. Pompey realised that any attempt to push the measure through would merely result in an humiliating defeat, and so he bided his time. At this moment the news of Lucullus' financial reforms in Asia provided him with powerful allies in the shape of the Equites. He had secured their affections by his reform of the jury-courts in this very year, and the two parties were now drawn still closer together by their common hatred of Lucullus. The stringent limitations he had imposed on their activities had hit them hard on their most tender spot—the pocket—and they were burning for revenge. Moreover, Pompey had already shown himself sympathetic to their interests. If he were in charge of the East, who could tell what concessions might be allowed to the order? Hence, impelled by the strong motives of revenge and self-interest, the Equites readily received Pompey's overtures. Some time in 69 the two parties came to an informal agreement to work for Lucullus' recall; and it was decided that for the present

Pompey should remain inactive until his opportunity came.

This alliance was the more valuable for Pompey in that the Equites, partly through his own reforms, had now become once more a political power in the State, and the Senate was willing to indulge their demands as far as it reasonably could in order to conciliate them. First, however, the ground must be prepared; and to this end the coalition (acting through the financial agents in Asia) probably suborned some of Lucullus' staff to stir up the latent discontent of his troops. Next came a more direct frontal attack on his position, for in 69 we find the province of Asia being transferred to a praetor, who actually took it over in the following year. The Senate acquiesced in this proposal, for it naturally wished to restore the *status quo* in the East as soon as possible; and it did seem as if the war-clouds had blown away from Asia for good. But it affected Lucullus in that it cut him off from one of his main sources of supply; and the jubilant coalition, to whom, if our hypothesis be correct, this proposal must be ascribed, could justly regard it as the thin end of the wedge.

The news of Lucullus' brilliant victory at Tigrano-certa seemed at first a decisive set-back for the allies. Lucullus' triumphant dispatches roused a temporary wave of patriotic, almost jingoistic, enthusiasm at Rome. But the Equites were not discouraged, and soon turned even this to account. They suggested that Lucullus had deliberately let the king escape so that he might remain a proconsul a little longer, and continue dragging the People into one war after another; he was accused of rank chauvinism, and of pursuing a policy of needless expansion. This was an ill-founded charge, but it was very telling in view of the strong objection of the Senate to any unnecessary increase in its responsibilities. At all events, the faith of the Senate in Lucullus gradually weakened, and the opinion gained ground that perhaps after all his powers should be circumscribed. This tendency was facilitated by the fact that many of the senators were themselves heavily indebted to members of the Equestrian order, and were therefore amenable to their influence. The restoration of the tribunate provided the Equites with another effective instrument for their agitation. The tribunes could act as mouthpiece for the carefully stimulated ill-feeling of the People towards Lucullus, and the Senate could no longer afford to disregard their opinion.

One of the leaders of the opposition to Lucullus was Lucius Quinctius, the praetor for 68, who had already, as tribune, crossed swords with him during the year of his consulate.[1] Now, at the beginning of 68, Quinctius proposed in the Senate that the consul for the year, Q. Marcius Rex, should take over the province of Cilicia from Lucullus. The Senate, moved by popular opinion, and with its own faith in Lucullus somewhat shaken, agreed to the proposal. Those senators who mistrusted this direct attack upon their own representative could console themselves with the thought that Lucullus retained Bithynia and Pontus, the two key provinces of the war. The former he had taken over from necessity

---

[1] Sallust tells us that Lucullus heard of Quinctius' intentions, and sent him a gift of money to induce him to keep silence (*h.* IV, 71). Whether Lucullus actually submerged his pride to such an extent is unknown, but if he did, it was in vain.

on the sudden departure of Cotta; the latter he had himself annexed to the Roman empire two years previously. The 'commission of organisation' had already departed from Rome, and from the point of view of administration the Senate now ranked Pontus with all the other provinces. Hence apologists for the measure might truly say that Lucullus had still as many provinces directly under his charge as in 74; but he was no longer the generalissimo of the whole of Asia Minor.

The Senate's decree instructed Marcius to leave for his province before the end of his year of office; perhaps too it specifically entrusted him with the conduct of a war against the pirates who infested the Cilician coastland. We find him claiming a triumph on his return to Rome in 63, and this could scarcely be for his services against Mithridates. His departure for the East was however delayed a little by Caesar's suspicious activity among the Transpadanes. The Senate feared that his agitation might lead to trouble, and ordered Marcius to remain in Italy until the affair had blown over. Perhaps he made a demonstration march through the affected region with the three legions he had been granted. At all events, peace was quickly restored, and by the spring of 67 Marcius arrived in his province.

Meanwhile alarming rumours began to reach Rome of discontent and sedition in the army. This ill-feeling was fostered by self-interested agitators such as the young Publius Clodius, the lieutenant and brother-in-law of Lucullus, who was discontented because the general very wisely refused to allow him special privileges. He ingratiated himself with the army, and organised mass-meetings where he attacked the general. Finally he rejected the authority of Lucullus, and fled to Cilicia, where he attached himself to the staff of the newly arrived governor, Marcius. It is fairly certain that this agitation was due as much to the prompting of the Equites as to a sense of personal injury.

Nor did the tale of Lucullus' Armenian expedition lose anything in the telling. An impartial observer in the capital might well ask how much longer he should be allowed to continue his wild-goose chase of Mithridates. Hence the ground was prepared for a *plebiscitum* of Aulus Gabinius Capito. Gabinius, an active and determined member of the popular party who had been elected to the tribunate for 67, introduced a law shortly after entering upon office by which the consul for the year, Manius Acilius Glabrio, should take over Lucullus' two remaining provinces of Bithynia and Pontus. At the same time it laid down that Lucullus' long tenure of command was an infringement of traditional custom;[1] and it ordered that the soldiers enlisted by L. Valerius Flaccus in 86 should be dismissed from the colours. This very comprehensive measure meant in effect the complete supersession of Lucullus, and was sure to be opposed. But Gabinius was a clever politician. He roused the popular feeling in the public meetings by lurid attacks on Lucullus; while he attempted to conciliate the Senate by nominating as Lucullus' successor a sound and loyal conservative, who was noted for his uprightness of character. The Assembly passed the bill with enthusiasm, and the Senate made no effort to block the law. Glabrio set out for his province immediately. As soon as he had landed he declared Lucullus' command to be at end; but

[1] *de imp. Cn. Pom.* 9, 26.

owing to his incapability it was autumn of the same
year before he finally took over the army from his
predecessor.

## THE *LEX GABINIA*

What, meanwhile, of Pompey? The proposal of Gabinius seems at first glance completely to neglect the
interests of the man whom we have seen to be the prime
force behind the anti-Lucullan movement. We might
have expected the provinces of Bithynia and Pontus to
have been handed over directly to him, instead of to a
representative of the Senate. But in the first place, to
have attempted to replace Lucullus by Pompey might
have roused the dormant corporate feeling of the Senate
to such an extent as to endanger the whole bill; and
secondly, Pompey was at this time aiming at other game.
At the beginning of 67 all other issues at Rome were
overshadowed by the pirate question. The depredations
of these pests had at last affected the corn supply. This
touched the Roman People nearly, and it was determined
to take active steps to suppress the pirates once for all.
Public opinion inclined towards the creation of one big
command, by which the pirates could be swept off the
seas. Pompey was not insensible of the glances thrown
in his direction. Such a command offered unexpected
possibilities. It was urgent, but the Eastern command
could wait. Lucullus, of course, must be recalled. He
was too dangerous a man to be left at large in the East,
and the popular feeling against him had been so success-
fully cultivated that it could no longer be restrained.
But if he were replaced by a nonentity, then Pompey
himself could step in at his leisure to finish off the war.

Such, we may imagine, were Pompey's thoughts.
Subsequent events make it scarcely too fanciful to suppose that he was acting in collusion with Gabinius
throughout, and that Glabrio was deliberately chosen,
without his own knowledge, to keep the place warm for
Pompey. Certainly, there could have been no better
choice; for while his known integrity lulled the Senate
into acquiescence, his constitutional laziness and in-
decision made his own replacement an easy matter when
the time came.

Hence we are not surprised to find the same Gabinius
following up his appointment of Glabrio by bringing
forward a bill to deal with the pirate problem. Perhaps,
indeed, both questions were dealt with in one and the
same law. In any case, they were closely connected in
the public mind.

This latest measure of the tribune, destined to go down
to history as the *Lex Gabinia,* provided for the appointment of an ex-consul with extraordinary powers to
suppress the pirates; Pompey was implied, but not
mentioned by name. The bill was opposed only by the
more extreme senators under Catulus and Hortensius,
who persuaded two tribunes to interpose their veto.
Gabinius countered by reintroducing the bill with still
broader provisions, and after some tension the Senate
yielded. Pompey was elected to the command by the
tribes, and confirmed in it by a decree of the Senate.[1]
His province was to consist of the whole Mediterranean,
with the coastland up to fifty miles inland. It was to last
for three years, and he was to have two quaestors, 24
legates, 500 ships, and up to 125,000 men. He was also

[1] Dio, xxxvi, 37.

granted 6000 talents from the Treasury. This command, with its sequel of the following year, is the most important landmark in the sequence of extraordinary commands which paved the way for the monarchy. Three points in connection with it deserve notice:

A. The institution of so many legates with praetorian power is significant. Moreover it was stated that Pompey should have the right of naming them himself. It is true that the Senate was probably left with the formality of confirming these appointments, and that Pompey did his best to conciliate it by choosing many of his lieutenants from the ranks of the 'conservatives'. Moreover he did not exert his privileges to the full, for we can only find traces of thirteen legates being actually appointed; one of his nominees, indeed, Gabinius himself, was rejected by the Senate. It is interesting to speculate whether Lucullus himself had pointed the way to this system of administration when he left C. Salluvius Naso as *legatus pro praetore* in Asia during his absence from the province.[1]

B. Pompey's command, although *infinitum*, was scarcely unlimited. He was granted *imperium pro consule*, but it was only *aequum*, and he had no power to over-ride the other consular governors even within his province. This anomalous position might, and did, lead to a conflict of competence which would be creditable to neither party.[2]

---

[1] *C.I.L.* xiv, 2218; an inscription found at Nemi. We know that Salluvius was active in Asia, and especially Mysia, from 74 onwards. Cf. the *legati Augusti pro praetore* who later became the regular governors of the imperial provinces.

[2] See Mommsen, *R.S.R.* ii (2), 654.

C. Mommsen suggests that the bill was opposed by the Equites as being too radical. His main evidence seems to be the coincidence that one of the tribunes who opposed the bill later introduced the *Lex Roscia*, which was designed to win over the Equites to the side of the Senate; but the two incidents are probably unconnected. Their own interests led the Equites to support the bill. The leaders of the order had been in close alliance with Pompey ever since his consulship, and they rightly regarded this command as the prelude to that greater command in the East which would enable him to open up new fields for their activity. Even the Senate itself was divided on the question, for many of the more moderate members, much as they disliked the manner of the proposal, yet approved of its aim in the interests of efficiency. Cicero mentions among its supporters Servilius, Curio, Lentulus and C. Cassius.

Pompey justified his appointment by sweeping the Mediterranean clear of pirates in an incredibly short time. While he was occupied in this task, things were going from bad to worse in Asia, and almost all the conquests of Lucullus had fallen back into the hands of the enemy. The time had come for decisive intervention. Accordingly Pompey concluded his campaign by rounding up the pirates of the Cilician coast, and established himself in winter-quarters in Cilicia while his agents at Rome got to work on his behalf. The fact that he did not return to Rome for the winter plainly shows that he anticipated service in Asia in the following year.

## THE *LEX MANILIA*

Once again it was through the medium of a friendly
tribune that Pompey attained his object. C. Manilius,
a demagogue of shady reputation, succeeded Gabinius
in the office at the end of 67, and early in the next year
he brought before the assembly the famous proposal to
be known as the *Lex Manilia*. This measure provided
that the present commanders in Asia be recalled, and
the four provinces, together with the conduct of the war
against Mithridates, be entrusted to Pompey.

Since he had handed over his troops to Glabrio in the
previous autumn, Lucullus had been in the anomalous
position of a general without an army, and a governor
without a province; for the appointment of Glabrio had
not, as Reinach suggests, affected either his *imperium*
or his general authority as commander-in-chief against
Mithridates. Now however he was to lose even the
semblance of power, and was to be recalled to Rome in
virtual disgrace. This was a direct attack not only on
him personally, but on the Senate which had sent him
to the East. Hence the measure was opposed both by
the kinsmen of Lucullus and by those senators such as
Catulus and Hortensius whose chief aim was the maintenance of the Sullan constitution.

The People on the other hand were enthusiastic for
the bill as being proposed by one of their own leaders.
Moreover Pompey had become the idol of the mob after
his brilliant exploits against the pirates. The Equites
too were favourable. This was the consummation of their
revenge upon Lucullus, while they placed high hopes in
their ally Pompey. It is unlikely that he had restored the

system of tithe-farming in Asia during his consulate; but his seizure of Syro-Cilicia in 67, although probably nothing more than a strategic move against the pirates, confirmed them in their belief that he would open up fresh fields for financial conquest. At the same time they were no more eager than the Senate to establish a military monarchy, and they were firmly resolved only to use Pompey as a tool for the moment. We may imagine the wealthy Crassus already wondering where the megalomania of his rival would end; but for the present it suited the interests of the Equites to let Pompey have the Eastern command for which they had jointly schemed ever since the alliance between the two parties had been sealed three years before.

Many of the less extreme senators were also in favour of the measure. The propaganda of the last two years had had such effect on them that they really thought Lucullus alone was responsible for the loss of the Roman conquests and the prolongation of the war. Moreover, Lucullus' unfortunate lack of affability towards the young nobles of his suite cannot have strengthened his position with their kinsmen at Rome.

Caesar, just back from Spain, was another strong supporter of the bill. Perhaps he foresaw that some day he would himself have to ask for such a grant of extraordinary power. Cicero, who had fallen under the spell of Pompey's personal charm, made his first political speech on behalf of the measure. Despite his studied compliments, he cannot conceal the fact that Lucullus is being recalled largely because of the ill-will of the Equites.

Such wide and influential support gave the bill an easy

passage. Even its opponents could not deny that the wide powers given to Pompey in the previous year had been justified by the use he made of them. The trust placed in him is shown by the fact that the status accorded to him by the new law was even higher than that of the *Lex Gabinia*. It was still *imperium aequum*, but he seems to have been granted special permission to make war and peace on his own responsibility.[1]

Tenney Frank states of this command that 'Pompey was the first general frankly sent out for the purpose of extending Rome's boundaries'; but the supporters of the measure were actuated rather by personal and practical motives than by any deep-founded imperialism. Pompey himself desired nothing more than an opportunity to display his 'indispensability'; his triumph was doubly sweet in that it involved the downfall of his old rival Lucullus.

In the early spring of 66 the not unexpected news of his appointment to the Eastern command reached Pompey in Cilicia. He accepted it with a show of reluctance which deceived nobody; even the guileless Plutarch characterises it as 'mere trifling'. His immediate activity shows that he had already prepared his plans in anticipation of the command. Within a few days of the receipt of his commission, he despatched messengers to all parts of Asia, to command the soldiers to join him in Cilicia, and to summon the tributary kings and princes to his councils. Presumably, too, he sent legates to take

[1] So Appian, *Mith.* 97; Appian may be exaggerating—but Dio deliberately styles Pompey's reluctance to wage war on Parthia without the Senate's permission a mere 'pretext' (πρόφασις) (Dio, xxxvii, 6, 7).

over the provinces of Bithynia and Asia; Pontus, of course, was still in the hands of the enemy.[1]

At the same time he issued an edict that he would recognise none of the arrangements made by Lucullus and his 'commission of ten'. There was no need to assert his supremacy so bluntly; but Pompey was always conspicuous for his lack of tact. His determination to reverse all his predecessor's decisions was not only petty but manifestly unfair to the people concerned. Strabo mentions that Pompey failed to confirm the honours promised to his grandfather,[2] and this was not the only case where faithful allies of Rome suffered through the personal rivalry of the generals.

Lucullus felt deeply the humiliation of his recall and supersession. Personally he had no wish to see his successor, but his staff thought that a conference might bring to an amicable ending what threatened to develop into an undignified squabble, and he was persuaded to accept their well-meaning suggestion. The two generals met in the Galatian fortress of Danala. The meeting opened with formal compliments, but feeling was too strong to be restrained within the bounds of frigid politeness. Compliment was succeeded by recrimination and recrimination by insult. Eventually the exchange became so violent that their staffs had to intervene, and the two generals parted after an interview which cast no credit on either of them.

Lucullus even now stubbornly refused to recognise

[1] These legates would have the same status of propraetor as his lieutenants in 67. Drumann has collected the names of five such *legati pro praetore* who served under Pompey in Asia during the years 66–64.

[2] Strabo, xii, 836.

Pompey's authority, and attempted to carry on with the organisation of the new provinces. This was a false move which put him in the wrong. As the thirty days' grace allowed to the retiring governor had now expired, Pompey had the letter of the law, as well as the legions, behind him. We can only suppose that Lucullus was so filled with bitterness that he was unable to see the realities of the situation. Pompey did not miss his chance to humble his rival still further. He formally forbade any notice to be taken of his orders, and he withdrew from him the few cohorts that had remained under his command in the previous autumn, leaving him a bare escort of 1600 men, and those the scum of the army, for his triumph. Finally, even Lucullus saw that the position was hopeless, and he sailed away to Rome with his raggle-taggle following.[1]

Such was the manner in which the three years' intrigue of Pompey and the Equites met with success. The question of the recall of Lucullus is still fraught with controversy. Ormerod[2] rightly declares that while 'Lucullus was the real conqueror of Mithridates', nevertheless 'the Roman government, whatever its motives, was right in superseding him'. There is no doubt that in 66 a change in the Eastern command was imperative. Mithridates had won back all his losses, and Lucullus was powerless to take the field against him. But the question at issue goes deeper. Granted that the recall of Lucullus eventually became a necessity, why had this situation arisen, and who was responsible for it?

[1] Yet even these rascals had their uses. Cicero tells us (*pro Mur.* 33, 69) that after taking part in Lucullus' triumph in 63 they just turned the scale for Murena at the consular elections.      [2] *C.A.H.* IX, 371.

In actual fact, the débâcle of Lucullus after the second Armenian campaign was due to a combination of causes, none of which would have been fatal by itself. We have stressed the part played by Pompey and the Equites, but their efforts would have been useless if the ground had not been ripe for them.

Lucullus himself was not entirely free from blame for his downfall. He did not allow for the weaknesses of his soldiers, and hence his plan of campaign, so brilliant in design, failed in execution. A workman cannot rise above his tools, and Lucullus placed too high a strain upon the very poor material on which he had to rely.

Still more culpable was the Senate. It showed a lamentable weakness in not putting a stop to the agitation against Lucullus at Rome, which it allowed to increase in strength and virulence until it was itself infected. Even more damaging was its failure to provide Lucullus with adequate support during the war. He did not want the money which, to do it justice, the Senate offered him for the purposes of the fleet. But he was in urgent need of men, and the Senate left him to carry on for eight years with his scratch lot of troops, all of whom, with the exception of one legion, had been taken over from previous commanders. If Lucullus had been sent two fresh legions in 70, he could have stiffened up his weakening forces, and he could even have afforded to dismiss some of his most troublesome troops. The confident tone of Lucullus' dispatches contributed to this neglect; for he was too proud to ask for help, and he placed an exaggerated reliance on his own power to keep his forces up to the mark. But the main cause of it was the propaganda of the Equites, which led Rome to think that the war was virtually over and was only being prolonged by Lucullus to satisfy his own ambitions.

After the first mutiny in 68 the Senate could have remedied the situation in two ways. It could have even then sent Lucullus two fresh legions, and ordered the dismissal of the restless *Fimbriani*; or it could have definitely instructed him to retire to Pontus, and be content with the consolidation of what he had already gained. Mithridates was an old man and could scarcely be a danger to Rome for much longer, while Tigranes had presumably had his lesson. The Senate took neither course. Instead of helping Lucullus it weakened him still further by allowing Gabinius to transfer his two remaining provinces to a man of straw. Lucullus was left without support. Mithridates pursued his reconquest of Pontus unhindered, and the next year the Senate was compelled to entrust Pompey with the task of recovering the lost ground. It was obvious that Lucullus in his present position could do nothing. The Senate, whether rightly or wrongly, dared not antagonise the Equites by restoring him to command and power. The only alternative was to recall him. The more practical senators saw this; it was only the rigid constitutionalists who objected to what was the one possible solution of a problem which should never have been allowed to arise.

A far-sighted spectator could have drawn two lessons from this impasse. The one was that the Senate had an exaggerated fear of its political associates, the Equites and the Populares. The other was that under the present military system, the relations between a general and his troops were of paramount importance. The soldiers depended on their general for everything, pay, discharge, and pensions. Is it too much to suppose that Caesar, watching events at Rome, drew the moral from them; and that in later years he remembered the fate of Lucullus, the man who could not rely on his army?

The remaining years of Lucullus' life were uneventful. The empty glories of a magnificent, if long-delayed, triumph could not reconcile him to his position. His supersession by Pompey still rankled, and he could not forgive his associates in the Senate for not making more efforts on his behalf. During his eight years' absence from Rome the political situation had changed so considerably that he felt lost in the maze of intrigue which now surrounded him. For both these reasons he felt disinclined to take an active part in the proceedings of the Senate; he had always had a desire for study and retirement, and now he could gratify his tastes. But his decision to retire from politics was only reached gradually, and although he consistently refused to lead the 'conservative' bloc in the Senate he was active in most of the major political crises of the next few years. He was especially to the fore whenever he saw an opportunity of striking a blow at his rival Pompey; and it was not until the closing years of his life that the feud was so far healed as to allow of friendly intercourse between the two generals.

Fabulous accounts of Lucullus' life in retirement have come down to us, but most of them must be discounted as gossip or exaggeration. He certainly lived in luxury, but he gave way neither to the license of Capri nor to the eccentricity of a Ludwig. Like many nobles of the day, he despaired of the commonwealth, and devoted himself to the art of living. He died in his sixty-first year, early in 56.[1] His death revived memories of his former successes, and a wave of popular feeling was aroused. Lucullus had never courted the common people in his lifetime, but now that he was dead all Rome, nobles and commons alike, realised that it had lost a great general and a great statesman.

## LUCULLUS: THE PROCONSUL OF THE SENATE

We have throughout this chapter regarded Lucullus as a loyal servant of the Sullan constitution, perhaps the most perfect exponent of his master's ideals; hence a short study of his aims and ideals may be of value. Ferrero[2] compares him to Alexander and Napoleon. Like the latter, 'he lived in a world of diplomacy which he tried to settle with the sword'. 'Pompey and Caesar were the two great pupils of Lucullus...he was the creator of the new imperialism.' But this thesis is scarcely borne out by the history of Lucullus' campaigns in the East. His reorganisation of Pontus was 'a work of political necessity';[3] the invasion of Armenia was due solely to strategical motives. The projected invasion of Parthia which Ferrero postulates has been adequately disproved. More positive evidence against Lucullus' 'imperialism' is provided by his treatment of Syria. By recognising the Seleucid claimant's title to the throne Lucullus signified his support of that traditional bulwark

[1] Cicero, speaking in June of 56, speaks of him as dead (*de prov. cons.* 9, 22).

[2] *Op. cit.* (Eng. trans.), I, 223.

[3] Tenney Frank, *Roman Imperialism*, p. 309; cf. Marsh, *Founding of the Roman Empire*, p. 70.[1]

of Roman policy, the client-kingdom; it is interesting to contrast Pompey's brusque rejection of Antiochus and annexation of his realm. But neither general was a conscious imperialist. Pompey, as we have seen above,[1] organised the East on practical lines without conscious reference to principles; his predecessor was a senator of the old school, with an innate mistrust of territorial expansion, and a deep respect for the dignity of kingship. His aim was to confirm and establish the peace of Rome in the East. His long and arduous campaigns against Mithridates, and his financial reorganisation of Asia, show a profound sense of responsibility and service. A man with such qualities might well be of more value to the State than the brilliant expansionist of Ferrero.

As in foreign affairs, so in the political world, Lucullus' aims have suffered misrepresentation. Gelzer compares him with Julius Caesar, to the advantage of the latter. Both generals were removed from office; but while Caesar dared to defy the order and arouse civil war, Lucullus had to comply with his recall. Now, it is true that Lucullus lacked Caesar's personal hold upon his soldiers, but this is not the only difference between the two cases. There were circumstances outside Lucullus' control which made it impossible for him to defy the Senate; the most obvious being the fact that he had no pacified Gaul at his back. But the real reason why Lucullus did not attempt to establish the military monarchy in his person lay in his steadfast loyalty to the constitution. A senator by birth, ideals and education, he could not turn traitor to his ideals even when he had himself been abandoned by the Senate. In the moment

[1] P. 54.

of his greatest provocation he might make a petty and ineffectual attempt to thwart his successor, but even if he had had the opportunity, he would never have dreamt of marching his legions on Rome.

Lucullus was unfortunate in his age, for his political ideals were over a century too old. Had he lived at a time when the supremacy of the Senate was unshaken, he would have had a long and honoured career in public life. But as it was, he was too disinterested to play for his own hand in the sordid game of contemporary politics; and he was not great enough to rally the Senate round himself so as to resist the challenge of the disruptive forces. Hence his career ended in failure. But he remains a figure of interest and importance to the historian for two reasons. The one is provided by his positive achievements, the other by the fact that in the story of his life we have the political history of the period in brief. His very retirement was representative of the *fin de siècle* attitude which prevailed at Rome. The best members of the Senate withdrew, with Lucullus, from public life; and enthusiasts like Cicero and Cato found few to support them in their hopeless efforts to ward off the military monarchy which we, from the elevation of two thousand years, can see to have been inevitable. But as long as he held public office, Lucullus did his duty to the State and the provinces; and a senator of Rome could desire no better epitaph.

## CHAPTER V

## THE ADMINISTRATION OF
## THE PROVINCES

W<small>E</small> have discussed the provincial and foreign policy
of the Senate, and we have shown how the appointment
to command was affected by political intrigue, such as
was seen at its worst in the career of Lucullus. Let us
now turn to the administration of the provinces, and the
relationship between the Senate and the Governor
during this period.[1]

The Roman governor occupied a position of unique
responsibility. The laudatory catalogue of Q. Cicero's
achievements in Asia[2] shows his wide powers for good
or ill. The Senate deliberately maintained the *dignitas
imperii*:[3] it is significant that Cicero can pride himself
on the unusual approachability he showed in Cilicia.

The governor united in himself several functions, for
the Roman, like the Englishman, mistrusted the special-
ist in government. He was the commander-in-chief of
the armies in the province, with the right to hold levies,
recruit veterans, or even demobilise his forces. In theory
he had absolute power of jurisdiction, although in
practice he was usually assisted by a council chosen from
the Roman citizens living in the province. He was
finally the supreme financial officer; for although the

---

[1] The standard authority for Roman provincial administration is still
W. T. Arnold's *Roman System of Provincial Administration*, to which
this chapter is largely supplementary.

[2] *ad Q.F.* 1, 1, 25.　　　　　　[3] *de prov. cons.* 8, 18.

routine of financial administration was delegated to a subordinate, it was the governor who decided how much money had to be remitted to Rome, and who controlled the currency of the province.[1]

At first sight it might appear that the governor's power was unlimited. Arnold cites the inadequacy of the Senate's control as a cardinal vice of provincial administration. It is true that on reading the Verrine Orations we may wonder how such a scoundrel managed to avoid condemnation for so long. There is no doubt that Verres richly deserved his fate, but a system does not stand condemned by one example of maladministration. In actual fact the authority of the governor was subject to very definite limitations, being restricted both from below, by his subordinates, and from above, by the Senate.

### THE INFLUENCE OF THE SUBORDINATE OFFICERS

The *Comites*, or unofficial 'secretaries of legation' (Arnold), can be briefly dismissed. They were supported at the public cost, but they were completely dependent for their appointment and advancement on the governor. They stood to him in the relation of personal friends,[2] and hence they would scarcely offer open opposition to his will; but the extent of their personal influence is shown by the care with which the litigant in Horace propitiates them.[3] Their duties were mainly nominal,

[1]  *ad fam.* III, 3, 2; Cicero hears that Appius is going to demobilise his army.  *pro Flacc.* 28, 67; Flaccus forbids the Jews of Asia to export gold to Jerusalem.

[2]  Caesar, *b.g.* I, 39, 2.                    [3]  *Satires,* I, 7.

and often they secured appointment merely in the hope
of sharing in the perquisites of the governor. Cicero
could justly pride himself on his refusal to share the
surplus of his chest with his 'cohort'. He attacked the
disreputable crowd that hung round Verres; Clodius
seems to have behaved no better when he was with
Murena in Gaul. On the other hand he can smile at
Trebatius, who hastened off to join Caesar with as high
hopes as if his letter of introduction were a banker's
draft.[1] The institution was not, however, without a
deeper value, for by acting as *assessor* the young Roman
noble acquired practical training in the art of jurisdiction.
At best such a lieutenant was of valuable help to an
overworked governor; at worst he was a burden to the
province, and a thorn in the flesh of a conscientious
superior.

The *Legati* were more important by reason of their
definite status and duties; they must be distinguished
from the *legati* sent on a special embassy to a province
or kingdom, although both offices had the same sanction.
In each case the *legatus* possessed authority from the
Senate. Hence it was a constitutional principle that the
choice of the legates should rest with that same body;
and Mommsen has good grounds for citing as a main
factor in the fall of the senatorial régime the fact that
the appointment of legates passed more and more to the
commanders themselves. In practice the commander's
wishes had for long been consulted. As early as 169 the
Senate commissioned the consul to choose legates for
Macedonia who should be acceptable to Aemilius. Verres
secured his appointment as legate to Dolabella by his

[1] *II in Verr.* ii, 10, 27; *de harus.* 20, 42; *ad fam.* vii, 7, 1.

own importunity.  Cicero could openly speak of 'choosing' his legates in Cilicia.  But such a concession was an
act of grace.  In 67 the *Lex Gabinia* specifically allowed
Pompey the right of choosing his own legates, but he
subjected his nominees to the Senate for ratification.
Hence Cicero can charge Vatinius with being the first
to take the right of nomination completely out of the
hands of the Senate.  Clodius saw to it that Gabinius and
Piso received the same privilege, and it was incorporated
in subsequent extraordinary commands as a matter of
course.[1]

Usually there were three legates to each consular
province, and one to a praetorian, but the number was
increased in special cases.  In 56 the Senate despatched
ten extra legates to Caesar in Gaul.  It has been suggested that these formed a senatorial commission to
organise the new province, but Rice Holmes has disproved this in one of his incisive appendices;[2] it seems
certain that the ten were merely supernumerary lieutenants sent out to work with Caesar.

Appointments were not as a rule limited to senators,
for Nepos remarks that Atticus had the chance of going
into Asia as legate under Q. Cicero.  The *Lex Gabinia*
specially restricted Pompey's choice to members of the
Senate in view of the praetorian *imperium* his legates
were to have.  Some restrictions were imposed by the
Licinian and Aebutian Laws, which forbade the appointment of anyone connected with the proposer of the
command.  Hence the Senate properly demurred at the
appointment of Gabinius as Pompey's legate in 67, and

[1] *II in Verr.* I, 16, 42; *ad fam.* XIII, 55, 1; *in Vat.* 15, 35.
[2] *Op. cit.* II, 294[2].

repeated its objections in the following year on the ground that the Manilian Law only continued the command granted the previous year. Gabinius did eventually serve in this capacity; but Cicero wilfully misunderstood the point at issue when pleading on his behalf. That he recognised and approved of the principle is shown by his attacks on Rullus and Vatinius in the same connection.[1]

The legate had power of jurisdiction in civil cases. He was not responsible to the governor for his actions, and any complaints against him had to be forwarded straight to Rome. Marquardt states that the governor had the power to dismiss the legate if he found him unsatisfactory; but the passage he cites does not definitely establish this point.[2] Cicero contrasts the indulgence shown by Verres to his good-for-nothing friends with the sternness of other governors, who have 'packed off their quaestors, legates, prefects, and tribunes' for misbehaviour; but he does not say that such an action is strictly legal. As the legate derived his authority directly from the Senate we can scarcely believe that the governor was entitled to dismiss him arbitrarily, although it may well be that righteous anger drove him to such a step in an extreme case.

If the number of appointments had been increased the position tended to become a sinecure. Certainly Cicero does not seem to have found his duties as legate of Pompey very onerous.[3] The exploits of Verres as legate of Dolabella show what potential harm lay in the com-

---

[1] *de imp. Cn. Pom.* 19, 57; *de leg. agr.* II, 9, 22; *in Vatin.* 15, 35.

[2] Marquardt, *Römische Staatsverwaltung*, p. 527; *II in Verr.* III, 58, 134.

[3] *ad Att.* IV, 2, 6.

bination of a bad legate and a weak governor. When he himself was governor, his own legates were of a different type. After trying in vain to moderate his caprices, they left him in disgust, with one exception; nor did the one who remained, P. Tadius, show himself a subservient tool. He deliberately avoided Verres; and proved so irksome to him that he was removed from the command of the fleet and given other employment. The attitude of these legates is illuminating as showing what the average senator thought of Verres.

One example will suffice to show the restraining influence of a good legate. One of Piso's legates in Macedonia was a C. Vergilius, otherwise unknown to us. Cicero says that it was only due to the intervention of this 'brave and upright man' that the most sacred shrines of the Byzantines were not sacked.[1]

The *Quaestor*, originally a financial officer, had become the general secretary and lieutenant of the governor. As a rule there was one to each province, but by an ancient custom there were two in Sicily. The quaestorship was an elective office, the first step on the *cursus honorum*. The governor did not choose his own quaestor but had him assigned by lot; it was left for Caesar and Pompey to break this custom by appointing their own quaestors.[2] Cicero later charges Antony with running off to Caesar on election 'without the lot, without a decree of the Senate, without legal authority'.[3]

Occasionally, instead of a quaestor, we find mention of a proquaestor. The title of *pro quaestore* was given either to a legate who was carrying out the duties of a quaestor who had died in office, or to an ex-quaestor

[1] *de prov. cons.* 4, 7.    [2] *ad Att.* VI, 6, 4.    [3] *Phil.* II, 20, 50.

who undertook a second term of duty if the number of available quaestors did not suffice for all the provinces.[1]

The quaestor had judicial authority in civil affairs, and the governor could also remit cases of greater importance to him. Cicero mentions the quaestor Caecilius as holding assizes at Lilybaeum; apparently his judgments were open to appeal to the governor, for we find Verres reversing his decisions with an unusual regard for justice. His military duties were primarily concerned with the commissariat but in case of need he could be entrusted with direct leadership in the field.[2]

The quaestor's main functions, however, remained financial. He received the grants from the Treasury and the taxes were paid through him. He settled payments on the authority of the governor; the minting of coins at the governor's behest formed part of his duties, and they were often inscribed with his name alone. At the end of his year of office he forwarded a full statement of his accounts directly to the Senate and this remained in the archives of the Treasury. When accusing Verres, Cicero was able to cite the accounts of his quaestorship in Gaul thirteen years before as documentary evidence.[3]

The relationship between the governor and the quaestor was peculiarly intimate, and often they were joined as much by personal affection as by the ties of office. Cicero paints an idyllic picture of the good feeling between Apuleius and Plancius in Macedonia, and he urges his own quaestor, Caelius Caldus, to give him an

[1] Marquardt, *op. cit.* pp. 528–9; *I in Verr.* 36, 91.

[2] *Phil.* x, 6, 13.

[3] *II in Verr.* III, 76, 177; *pro Flacc.* 19, 44; Mommsen, *R. Münz.* 5, 374; *II in Verr.* I, 14, 36.

opportunity of strengthening their bonds by mutual intercourse.[1] The quaestor shared the responsibility of his superior, and in return the governor was in duty bound to consult him on any important matter.[2] Cicero rhetorically styles him 'guard not only of the chest but of the consul, his partner in all action and counsel'.[3] The governor was not, of course, obliged to take the advice of his inferior, but he naturally tended to treat him with respect; for as the latter was usually the scion of a noble house just entering public life, he had powerful friends at Rome and in the Senate to protect his interests. The power of a good quaestor is shown by the lasting influence of P. Sestius in Macedonia. Even if we discount Cicero's praises, yet his 'extraordinary integrity'[4] does seem to have left its mark.

We have seen above[5] that in an emergency the quaestor could take over the functions of the governor, with the rank of *quaestor pro praetore*. Sometimes, too, a quaestor was deliberately sent out to a province instead of a propraetor. Thus Lentulus Marcellinus was sent to be the first governor of Cyrene in 74 and Cato went to Cyprus as *quaestor cum iure praetorio* in 58. Such appointments, however, were extraordinary, and stood apart from the regular provincial appointments.[6]

[1] *pro Planc.* 11, 28; *ad fam.* II, 19, 1.
[2] *Div. in Caec.* 10, 32; *II in Verr.* v, 44, 114.
[3] *II in Verr.* I, 15, 40.          [4] *pro Sest.* 5, 13.
[5] *Supra*, p. 82; see also Marquardt, *op. cit.* p. 530.
[6] Among lesser officials may be mentioned the *Praefecti*. Their duties were mainly military, but the *negotiatores* sometimes obtained such appointments to buttress their own authority (*v. infra*, p. 191). They were appointed by the governor and must be distinguished from the prefects to whom the Senate granted small independent commands (see Arnold, *op. cit.* p. 68).

## THE RELATIONS BETWEEN THE SENATE
## AND THE GOVERNOR

The governor owed his appointment to the Senate, and he hoped to continue his career under its auspices; hence he did his best to keep on good terms with it. Moreover, his tenure of office largely depended on that same body, for he held his province as long as it was not 'named' by the Senate for the next year.[1] In 56 Cicero urged that Syria and Macedonia be allotted to the consuls for 55, to ensure the recall of his enemies Gabinius and Piso. Conversely it was his task to persuade the Senate not to 'name' the Gallic provinces which Caesar wished to retain. It has been suggested that M. Juncus was arbitrarily recalled from Asia for incapacity in 74, to make way for Lucullus. In 56 Cato proposed that Lentulus be superseded in Cilicia. This was a party move, because Cato was opposed to the suggestion that Lentulus should be entrusted with the restoration of Ptolemy, and Cicero warmly styles it 'disgraceful'.[2] Manutius has conjectured that Cicero was behind a proposal for the summary recall of Crassus from the East;[3] the question of Caesar's supersession occupied the attention of the Senate throughout 50.

The Senate was the sole source of honour. It was the ambition of every governor to have a supplication awarded in his honour even if he did not aspire to the higher glory of a triumph. He could only achieve his

---

[1] Of course governors were not always anxious to remain in their provinces, so this factor sometimes had little weight.

[2] *ad fam.* 1, 5a, 2: *nefaria.*

[3] From *ad fam.* v, 8, 1.

aim through the Senate, for both distinctions were awarded through its decrees. A good 'party' man might be granted a triumph on very flimsy grounds. Within the space of a few years, Cn. Dolabella, C. Curio and M. Lucullus were all awarded triumphs for their services in Macedonia.[1] Pomptinus received the same honour in 54 for his insignificant successes over the Gallic tribes, despite the opposition of the praetors Cato and Servilius. In 55 Cicero wrote that Lentulus' application would be successful; once again Cato tried to block it, but he only succeeded in postponing it for four years.[2] Even Bibulus was awarded first a supplication of extraordinary duration, and later a triumph; much to the disgust of Cicero, who did not rate his military successes very highly. His annoyance was aggravated when he found his own application baulked by the egregious Cato, and the latter's cold letter of consolation and explanation failed to satisfy his wounded pride. The Roman Senate was too jealous of Cicero to be ungrudging in its appreciation of his services.

If the Senate could thus refuse the request of one of its own supporters, it had no hesitation in denying the award to a governor who had made himself obnoxious by his independence or his maladministration. When Albucius, the governor of Sardinia, forwarded his application it was revealed that he had already held a mock triumph in his province; the Senate promptly refused him even the lesser honour. Gabinius sent frequent reports to the Senate in the hopes of a supplication, but a crowded house declared that it attached no credence

[1] *in Pis.* 19, 44.
[2] *ad fam.* 1, 8, 7; *ad. Att.* v, 21, 4.

to his dispatches, and would certainly not accede to his request. On the other hand the extraordinary supplications granted in Caesar's honour show that the Senate recognised meritorious services even in one of its opponents. It was seldom that the Senate descended to such petty manœuvring as when it burked Caesar of his triumph in 60, and even then it had the letter of the law on its side. The fact that it was expected that he would forgo the consulate rather than his triumph shows the value usually attached to such an honour.[1]

A governor was influenced also by fear of punishment. The *quaestiones* established or confirmed by Sulla covered amongst other crimes, treason, extortion and peculation, and the scope of the courts was further extended by the *Lex Julia*. In theory the provincials had ample protection against misgovernment; but the system of jurisdiction at Rome was deeply affected by the absence of two things, a permanent judicial bench, and a public prosecutor.

Each court was under the charge of a praetor, but he was merely the president of a large panel of jurymen. Gracchus had entrusted these panels to the Equites, Sulla to the Senate, and it is difficult to say which system was less satisfactory. Cicero, speaking as an Eques, thinks that the Gracchan juries were less corrupt, and produces a damning list of the abuses of the Sullan courts. It was said that it cost £30,000 to get a governor condemned, while some senators took bribes

---

[1] Minor officials shared in the distribution of honours. On his return a governor forwarded to the Treasury what Tyrrell well styles a 'Resignation Honours List' of deserving subordinates. Cf. *ad fam.* v, 20, 7 and *pro Arch.* 5, 11.

from each side impartially.[1] Appian is equally definite in favour of the senatorial juries, and they were probably no worse than their predecessors.[2] The condemnation of Rutilius Rufus in 92 was even more disgraceful than the acquittal of Cn. Dolabella in 77 and of Opimius in 74. However, a reform was urgently needed, and the new system of 70 met with the approval even of a conservative like Catulus. In future the juries were to be drawn from three equal panels, composed respectively of senators, Equites and the so-called *tribuni aerarii*. The exact definition of the last two classes is uncertain, but it does seem that the different interests were now fairly represented in the law-courts.[3] Cases of injustice still occur, but on the whole there was much less spirit of class favouritism in evidence.

In the absence of a public prosecutor charges were left to private initiative. This put obvious difficulties and dangers in the way of dissatisfied provincials, but they were helped by the eagerness of the young Roman noble to undertake one of these accusations in the hope of making a name for himself. Moreover, once the case was started the plaintiff was under the protection of the court, and was granted power to collect evidence in the province in question. The facilities offered him are shown by the activity which Cicero displayed in Sicily, when he was building up a case against Verres.

A danger of this system lay in the scope it offered for personal and party feeling. Cicero declares that the prosecution of Flaccus was entirely due to the ill-will of Pompey, while M. Aemilius Scaurus was deliberately

---

[1] *I in Verr.* 13, 38.    [2] App. *bell. civ.* I, 22.
[3] The question is discussed by Last, *C.A.H.* IX, 339.

charged with extortion in Sicily in 54 to prevent him standing for the consulship. It meant however that it was almost impossible for a governor to avoid prosecution by concealing the evidence. His only chance lay in securing acquittal, by any means; and the practice of judicial corruption flourished even after the reform of the courts. But it was condemned by public opinion and never attained the prevalence supposed by Cicero in his speeches; when he says that the law-courts were positively injurious to the provincials, he is guilty of a gross misrepresentation.

Nor did the Senate remain in careless ignorance of a governor's activity, for he was expected to keep in touch with it by means of formal dispatches. In these he reported his own doings to the Senate, and also expressed criticisms and complaints. Mommsen suggests that he was only obliged to report military operations, and maintains that Cicero's dispatches from Cilicia were throughout nothing but field reports; but the Parthian danger was acute enough to warrant Cicero's concentration upon it, while he had the not infrequent tendency of the scholar to dwell the more upon his active triumphs. Evidence is scanty, but it does seem that a governor had to send dispatches to Rome even in peace time; although in the absence of military operations there would naturally be less extraordinary incident to report.

Pompey's famous dispatch from Spain in 75 [1] attained all the importance of a historical document, while Lucullus sent home similarly weighty reports. His praise of Murena's services was retained in the State archives; after his naval victory off Tenedos his dispatches were

[1] Sall. *hist.* II, 98.

'wreathed in laurel'.[1] Pompey sent in an official report of the suppression of the pirates which was read in the Senate; his letters announcing his impending return caused consternation at Rome.[2] Even Caesar realised that it was his duty to keep the Senate well posted about his doings; that Clodius was able to pass off forged letters from him in the Assembly shows that such reports were frequent.[3] Suetonius tells us that some of his genuine letters were extant in his own day; he adds that Caesar was the first to send his dispatches written out in book form.

Cicero, as we might expect, reported his campaigns in great detail. He explains to Cato that he has omitted to send formal information of certain events only because he believed Bibulus would have already reported them; he was to discover later how risky it was to let his reputation rest upon the correspondence of others.[4] He censures Verres for not reporting signs of incipient unrest in Sicily, and charges Piso with neglecting to write to the Senate. Gabinius, on the other hand, bombarded the Senate with reports of false victories until all faith in his letters was destroyed. His expedition to Egypt, however, he never reported at all, leaving it to be announced at Rome by popular rumour.[5]

As instances of dispatches to Rome of a less military character may be cited M. Aurelius Cotta's complaints

[1] Plut. *Luc.* 26; *pro Mur.* 9, 20; App. *Mithr.* 77.
[2] *de prov. con.* 11, 27; *ad fam.* v, 7, 1.      [3] *de dom.* 9, 22.
[4] *ad fam.* xv, 3, 2; ii, 17, 7: 'Bibulus in his dispatches appropriates all the glory to himself'.
[5] *II in Verr.* v, 4, 9; *de prov. con.* 6, 14; Dio, xxxix, 59. Note especially *in Pis.* 38: *Quis umquam provinciam cum exercitu obtinuit, qui nullas ad senatum litteras miserit?*

to the Senate about his quaestor Oppius, which led to the latter's recall, and Metellus' letters about the taxation of Sicily. These letters were addressed to Cn. Pompeius and M. Crassus the consuls, M. Mummius the praetor, and the urban quaestors respectively, and contained official notification of the fact that he had restored the Hieronic system of taxation.[1]

The governor had from the earliest times been accompanied by a senatorial committee composed of his legates and any other senators who happened to be on the spot. A late inscription[2] mentions six of these *assessores* in Sardinia. A governor was supposed to refer all important questions to this council, although this was not legally established; and Verres in Sicily could act on his own authority even when a defendant petitioned for the advice of the assessors to be taken into consideration. Cicero granted Ariobarzanes an audience in the presence of his council. At the outbreak of the Civil War Pompey was acting constitutionally when he consulted his council of senators.[3]

The council could bid the governor remit a matter of vital importance to the judgment of the Senate at Rome. Cicero with his usual fear of responsibility was only too willing to pass on his problems. That a more independent governor was not above seeking advice is shown by Cicero's reference to his brother Quintus. 'I want you to notice what he says about the customs', he writes to Atticus.[4] 'He is uncertain about the status of goods

---

[1] Dio, xxxvi, 40; *II in Verr.* iii, 53, 123.
[2] *C.I.L.* x, 7852.
[3] *II in Verr.* ii, 30, 75; *ad fam.* xv, 2, 5; *ad Att.* vii, 7, 4.
[4] *ad Att.* ii, 16, 4.

which are re-exported before being taken out of bond, and informs me that he has referred the matter to the Senate on the advice of his council. If any Greeks from Asia have come to Rome on this matter will you please give them my opinion?'

Sometimes, too, the Senate issued express instructions to the governors. In 70 envoys from Sicily prayed the Senate to forbid the erection of statutes to Verres during his governorship, and to ordain that the taxes be collected according to the *Lex Hieronica*. A clause in the *Lex de Termessibus*, which was perhaps passed in the same year,[1] lays it down that no Roman magistrate shall quarter his troops in the town or allow them to winter there 'unless the Senate has expressly decreed this'. We find also rescripts of universal application. The maladministration of Verres roused so much feeling at Rome that the consuls for 72 passed a special law that no one should be put on trial for a capital charge in his absence, and this was to have force in all the provinces; this measure met with the unanimous approval of the Senate.

The Senate did not allow the governor to make any alterations in the constitution on his own responsibility. One of the charges against Verres was that he had altered the laws of the province of Sicily *sine senatus auctoritate*. Clodius roused Cicero's anger by giving Piso control over the cities of Achaia, which had been freed by many decrees of the Senate. Elsewhere Cicero mentions a motion in the Senate to reimpose a tribute on certain states which had bought their freedom from Sulla;

[1] The date of the *Lex Antonia de Termessibus Maioribus* is discussed by Last, *C.A.H.* IX, 896, note 3.

neither the urban nor the provincial magistrates could do so on their own authority.[1]

Such were the factors and principles which governed the relations between the Senate and its deputy. It remains to consider more particularly what control the Senate exerted over the governor in the three main branches of his work, the financial, the military and the judicial.

## FINANCIAL CONTROL

The governor's financial relations with the Senate began even before he left Rome, for he was entirely dependent upon it for his official allowance, the *ornatio provinciae*. In 58 this was actually settled before the consuls took office, an innovation which displeased the scrupulous Cicero (who was impatient for his recall to Italy) but had the useful effect of preventing some of the jobbery which might attend the business. Only the consul could take money from the Treasury without a decree of the Senate[2] and hence the governor had to stay in Rome until the bill was passed. Mucius Scaevola paid his own expenses in Asia, and a rich ex-consul like Appius Claudius might threaten to dispense with it, and set out for Cilicia *sine sumptu*, but the importance usually attached to the grant is shown by the subterfuges to

[1] *II in Verr.* III, 7, 17; *de offic.* III, 22, 87.

[2] Zonar. VII, 13. That this was a fundamental principle at Rome is shown by Polybius (VI, 13, 2): οὔτε γὰρ εἰς τὰς κατὰ μέρος χρείας οὐδεμίαν ποιεῖν ἔξοδον οἱ ταμίαι δύνανται χωρὶς τῶν τῆς συγκλήτου δογμάτων πλὴν τὴν εἰς τοὺς ὑπάτους· τῆς τε παρὰ πολὺ τῶν ἄλλων ὁλοσχερεστάτης καὶ μεγίστης δαπάνης, ἣν οἱ τιμηταὶ ποιοῦσιν εἰς τὰς ἐπισκευὰς καὶ κατασκευὰς τῶν δημοσίων κατὰ πενταετηρίδα, ταύτης ἡ σύγκλητός ἐστι κυρία, καὶ διὰ ταύτης γίνεται τὸ συγχώρημα τοῖς τιμηταῖς.

which he and his colleague resorted to obtain it.[1]  It was only the fear of prosecution which led Caesar to leave for Spain without awaiting it in 61.

These grants were variable in amount and depended on the needs of the moment.  If military operations were in prospect they were considerably increased.  The large sums allotted to Caesar in 59 were more justifiable than the similar grant to Piso, which was due to the intervention of a tribune.  But the Senate itself was usually generous enough, even for a peaceful province.  Cicero was enabled to return a large part of his allowance to the Treasury at the end of the year; 'Now, I thought this course was both just and exemplary', he writes to Atticus,[2] 'that I should leave some of my allowance with my quaestor Caelius, and return up to a million sesterces to the Treasury.  But my suite was most indignant, thinking it ought to have been divided amongst it; in which case I should obviously have been showing more consideration to the local exchequer than to our own.'  A less scrupulous governor would not have treated the surplus in this way.  It was not unknown for a governor to divert some part of his allowance to private purposes, or even to invest it for himself before leaving Rome.  Cicero charges Piso with putting away no less than eighteen million sesterces before leaving for Macedonia.  He may well refer to the 'flourishing fortunes' of the general, and the strain thus inflicted on the Treasury;[3] but embezzlement on this scale must have been rare.

The grant was either paid directly or credited by the

[1] *ad Att.* IV, 18, 2.                    [2] *ad Att.* VII, 1, 6.
[3] *in Pis.* 35, 86; *ib.* 16, 37.

urban quaestors to the governor. Sallust mentions a quaestor who had 'conveyed the allowance to Marius in Africa'.[1] Cicero was interested to know whether his brother was to be paid in denarii or by a draft on Pompey's *cistophoroi* stored up in Asia to the credit of the government. In the latter case he would suffer from the depreciation of the currency. Eventually the grant was paid direct to Cicero in his brother's name; and he seems to have used some of it himself before forwarding it. When he himself went to Cilicia he received a bill which he cashed on arrival.[2]

Mommsen supposes that after the initial grant the Senate made no further allowances, but merely paid the wages of the legionaries. Unless however the governor were unusually spendthrift he had no difficulty in balancing his budget, despite the lack of a fixed salary. He could always divert some portion of the taxes to meet the cost of local administration; during the Civil War Cicero formally proposed that Brutus be empowered to use all public moneys he could lay his hands on for military purposes. A senatorial decree could also authorise the governor to borrow money from friendly states.[3]

But these expedients were rarely necessary in view of the many sources of income which a governor could tap. Apart from illegal requisitions there was the more or less open share which he received in any booty. The principle that all booty belonged to the State was maintained in theory until the end of the Republic,[4] but there

---

[1] *Jug.* 104.
[2] *ad Att.* II, 6, 2; *ad Q.F.* I, 3, 7; *ad fam.* III, 5, 4.
[3] *ad Brut.* II, 6, 1.     [4] Cf. Plut. *Pomp.* 4.

were certain established methods of diverting it from the Treasury. Donatives to the soldiers reached incredible proportions. Scipio had given each man 400 asses after the fall of Carthage, but this sum cannot be compared with the 6000 sesterces of Pompey or the 20,000 of Caesar; Pompey distributed 1600 talents in all by this means. Even Cicero admits to Atticus that after the capture of one town he surrendered the booty to the soldiers. The idea also developed that certain parts of the loot were the perquisite of the general, and these were entrusted to a separate officer to look after. Moreover, since the general had not to render accounts for the disposal of the booty,[1] it was not, like the other sources of his income, under the superintendence of the quaestor. Not every governor could, or would, emulate Verres, and seize a captured pirate ship for himself lock, stock and barrel, but we repeatedly find Roman generals being influenced by desire for booty. This constituted a grave weakness in the financial control exerted by the Senate over the governor; Cicero even speaks of *ad hoc* quarrels picked with rich cities for the sake of the booty.[2]

The *Leges Juliae* of 59 incorporated one of the most effective financial checks upon the governor. Henceforth the quaestor's accounts were to go through the governor, who was to be jointly responsible for them. On retiring he was to leave copies in at least two cities of his province, and deposit a duplicate in the Treasury for public inspection. It was a heavy charge against Piso that he had neglected to fulfil his duties in this respect. In 56 Metellus Nepos was so anxious to comply with the regulations that he sent his accounts from Spain to

[1] Mommsen, *R.S.R.* II, 530.    [2] *de imp. Cn. Pom.* 22, 65.

Cicero to be audited.[1]  Bibulus, of course, could not accept the validity of the law.  Cicero humours him by not pressing the point, but reminds his proquaestor Sallustius that this does not absolve him too from the duty of sending accounts.[2]  He himself was most scrupulous in this respect.  He carefully revised his quaestor's accounts and refused to publish them until he had passed them.  Cato showed the same diligence in preparing the accounts of his settlement of Cyprus.  It was one of the greatest blows of his career when both copies were lost; for there is nothing to support Tyrrell's unkind suggestion that the bottom of the sea may have been the best place for them.[3]

This institution served much the same purpose as the Athenian *euthuna*; although formulated by Caesar it was supported by all classes and is often praised by Cicero.[4]

### MILITARY CONTROL

The Senate had a very justifiable fear of concentrating too much power in the hands of one man.  It was a cardinal principle that no governor should go outside his province in arms without the express permission of the Senate.  The *Lex Cornelia de maiestate* postulated any such activity as treason, and this law became the sanction of the constitution.  It was confirmed by the *Lex Julia de repetundis* which forbade the governor to conduct diplomatic relations, to wage war, or to cross the frontier on his own responsibility.  This law was usually obeyed owing to the publicity which attended any breach of it,

[1] *ad fam.* v, 3.
[2] *in Pis.* 25, 61; *ad fam.* ii, 17, 2.
[3] *Op. cit.* iii, xxvi.
[4] See, e.g., *pro Sest.* 66, 135.

and it was rarely transgressed with impunity. Even authorised expeditions were liable to be misunderstood and criticised. Dio mentions a canard that Caesar's campaign against Ariovistus was illegal and undertaken to further his own ambition.[1] He also states, and Plutarch implies, that Crassus' invasion of Parthia was not sanctioned by the Senate. As early as 134 Aemilius Lepidus had been recalled from Spain for deliberately attacking the Vaccaei against the instructions of the Senate.[2] In 89 M'. Aquilius provoked the First Mithridatic War by inciting Nicomedes, on his own responsibility, to attack Mithridates. Murena had no more authority when he invaded Mithridates' territory in 83. He was granted a triumph, but Sulla did not conceal his displeasure. Such examples were infrequent; Verres' requisition of timber from Rhegium, a town outside his province, is venial in comparison.

The best evidence for the law is provided by the Egyptian imbroglio. After granting Lentulus authority to restore Ptolemy the Senate reversed its decision.[3] Lentulus applied to Cicero for advice, and his reply is one of sound common-sense.[4] He has talked the matter over with Pompey and they have decided that the vague decrees of the Senate may be neglected. Lentulus' authority in the matter had never been formally revoked, and he would be justified in occupying Egypt if a suitable occasion arose; but it would be wiser not to let Ptolemy return until the country had been thoroughly pacified. By this concession to public opinion he would avoid restoring the king 'with an army', that is, with

---

[1] Dio, xxxviii, 35, 2.  [2] App. *Hisp.* 81.
[3] See above, chap. ii, fin.  [4] *ad fam.* i, 7, 4.

the multitude so expressly forbidden by the Sibylline
oracle. Above all, he must not risk the chance of a
failure, and must only make the attempt if assured of
success. Meanwhile, however, Gabinius had occupied
Egypt from Syria. Cicero later defended Gabinius very
grudgingly; in attacking Piso he roundly declared that
no one in his right senses would have dared to transgress
such fundamental statutes as the *Lex Cornelia* and the
*Lex Julia*.[1]

It was equally unconstitutional for a governor to enter
the province of another. When Verres was proceeding
to Cilicia as Dolabella's legate he passed through the
province of Asia; and in sampling the pleasures of the
country he raised such a hornet's nest that he was compelled to send urgent messages to Dolabella to come to
his aid. Dolabella entered the province and persuaded the
governor Nero to entrust him with the settlement of the
matter. Verres' opponent was condemned and his own face
was saved. Cicero regrets the weakness shown by Nero,
and declares that Dolabella's conduct was reprehensible.[2]

Only the exigencies of military operations, it seems,
could over-ride this rule. If a province was faced by
serious war the Senate might authorise two governors
to co-operate, as Metellus and Pompey did in Spain; or
a governor could invite a colleague to his help. Bibulus
authorised his legates and quaestor to invite Cicero into
the province to help him to deal with the invading
Parthians.[3] Cicero was gratified by the implied compliment and agreed so far as to move his army over the
border nearer the enemy. But he would certainly never
have entered Syria without a definite invitation.

[1] *in Pis.* 21, 50.    [2] *II in Verr.* I, 29, 72 ff.    [3] *ad Att.* VI, 5, 3.

## JUDICIAL CONTROL

The administration of justice in the provinces rested on two main pillars. The first of these was the *lex provinciae*, drawn up by a senatorial commission upon the annexation of a province, and usually called after the general responsible for its conquest or organisation. We find the *Lex Mummia* in Achaia and the *Lex Rupilia* in Sicily; the *Lex Pompeia* was still the sanction in Bithynia in the time of the younger Pliny. By it the taxes were equitably proportioned, and the districts marked out. It regulated the relation between the local codes of law and the Roman, and defined the privileges of the free cities and states. Arnold thinks that there was no definite obligation on the part of the governor to maintain it; but Cicero's indignation at Verres' breaches of it seems to show that by the last fifty years of the Republic at any rate it had an absolutely binding force. Its very name Law shows its authority; few governors would dare to transgress it openly.

The *lex provinciae* did not in itself provide a whole code of law. Hence each governor, on entering office, published an edict in which he laid down the principles he would adopt, just as did the urban praetors at Rome. A large part of the edict became traditional under the name of *edictum tralaticium*,[1] and formed the nucleus of a fixed legal code. Cicero mentions that the slave law of M'. Aquilius has been adopted by every subsequent governor of Sicily. The Senate especially commended Scaevola's edict in Asia to the attention of his successors, and Cicero largely followed its provisions

---

[1] *ad Att.* v, 21, 11.

in Cilicia.[1] Like most governors, he composed his edict
before leaving Rome, and only made slight alterations
in it subsequently at the request of a deputation of tax-
gatherers. Bibulus' edict was, according to Atticus,
unfair to the Equites; Verres on the other hand granted
the order exceptional privileges in Sicily.

This 'system of law based on experiment' was on the
whole very successful. It combined continuity with
flexibility, for each governor could adapt his edict to
suit the time. It enabled him to make his principles
known before entering the province, and it provided the
provincials with a standard to which they might appeal.
The final step in the development of the system came in
67, when a *Lex Cornelia* laid it down that 'the praetors
should administer justice in accordance with their permanent edicts'. This was the formulation in words of a
custom that had become more and more fixed; for three
years before Cicero speaks of Verres' neglect of it as
extraordinary.[2]

Subject to the limits laid down by the *lex provinciae*
and his own edict, a governor's power of jurisdiction
was in theory almost unlimited. But it was the custom
to remit to Rome all cases where a citizen had to face a
capital charge; and it was even held advisable for a
governor to submit to the Senate any case of grave
political import, whatever the status of the defendant.
The Senate might also instruct the consuls to summon
the persons concerned to Rome. Cicero quotes the case
of an eminent Ephesian who was summoned to Rome to

[1] *II in Verr.* v, 3, 7; Val. Max. viii, 15, 5.
[2] *II in Verr.* i, 46, 119. The Provincial Edict has recently been discussed by W. W. Buckland in the *Revue Historique* (1934, p. 81).

stand his trial for treason at the request of Aurelius
Scaurus, a legate in Asia, and enquires why Verres has
not asked for similar action to be taken as the result of
an *émeute* at Lampsacus. Later, in 46, he himself re-
quested Ser. Sulpicius, the governor of Achaia, to refer
to Rome a case in which a senator was concerned, supporting his request by a consular rescript which perhaps
had the force of a command.[1]

Moreover, the absolute authority of the governor
over the provincial was tempered by two considerations.
Many of the provincials enjoyed the rights of Roman
citizenship; and the well-known case of Marcellus and
the magistrate of Novum Comum shows well enough
that the citizenship did as a rule provide some protection
against the excesses of a governor. A Roman citizen
was by law exempt from degrading punishments such
as scourging, and Cicero becomes lyrical in his indignation when he contemplates the enormity of Verres'
treatment of a Roman citizen like Gavius.[2]

But the franchise was as yet a jealously guarded
privilege, which applied only to a small proportion of
the provincials. Others, as residents in a free city,
would be protected by the special privileges defined in
the *lex provinciae*. The remainder had a safeguard
against oppression in the institution of patronage. Just
as a *cliens* at Rome had been protected by a *patronus*, so
could a provincial, or even a whole town or nation, rely
on the protection of some great Roman. A dependent
prince might enter into a similar relationship. As early

---

[1] *II in Verr.* I, 33, 85; *ad fam.* XIII, 26, 3.
[2] *II in Verr.* v, 66, 170: *facinus est vincire civem Romanum; scelus,
verberare; prope parricidium, necare; quid dicam, in crucem tollere?*

as 171 a Spanish embassy of complaint was directed by
the Senate to name four patrons to represent its interests. Gradually the theory developed that the first
conqueror of a nation became its patron;[1] thus Marius
was patron of the Gaetulians, Fabius of Transalpine
Gaul, Marcellus of Sicily, Cato the elder of Spain, and
his grandson of Cyprus. Often this relationship was
hereditary; the Gaetulians supported Caesar as representing the house of Marius; Pompey could rely on the
colonies in Cisalpine Gaul founded by his father. Sometimes official association was enough to establish such
relations; or a state might even attach itself to some
great man without any prior claim on him.

However the 'patronage' arose, the implications of
the bond were clearly recognised on both sides. The
patron exercised a general supervision over the welfare
of his client in the province. Merely to be known as the
client of a family like the Catones was sufficient to protect
a provincial from gross ill-treatment. Cicero writes to
Sulpicius to commend to him as governor the state of
the Lacedaemonians. He thought it his duty to inform
Cato of the Armenian invasion into Cappadocia because
of his relations with that nation. If a state sent an embassy to Rome, its interests would be forwarded by its
patron. Thus we find the envoys of the Allobroges taking
their troubles to their patron Fabius Sanga in 63. Individual clients were protected in the courts and shown
hospitality if they came to Rome. From Clodius' inquiry
whether Cicero had allotted the Sicilians special seats at
the games may be seen how far this interest extended.[2]

[1] This theory is formulated by Cicero (de offic. I, 11, 35).
[2] ad Att. II, 1, 5.

In return the clients granted their patrons special honours, and in case of need they were expected to render practical help; it was because they were his clients that the Transpadanes followed Caesar in the Civil War. Caesar himself realised the potential importance of this relationship when he was drawing up the charter of his colony of Genetiva Julia in Spain; for in this he ordained that no senator should become its patron unless he were a private citizen.[1] Its value to the provincials is shown by the fate of Tenedos, which lost its autonomy in 54 simply because, as Cicero admits, it had no patron to watch over its interests, and had to rely on the lukewarm support of one or two disinterested senators. Most important to the individual was the fact that if he appeared before the Roman governor he was defended by the name of his patron just as the client at Rome was by his presence.

\*     \*     \*     \*

From the above considerations it appears that the authority of the governor was by no means as great, in practice, as might be thought at first sight. It was circumscribed by the direct and indirect control of the Senate, by the influence of subordinate officials, and by the rights and privileges of the provincials themselves. The governor had great and perhaps excessive power, but to represent him as omnipotent for good and ill is an exaggeration.

There remain two important questions which may well be discussed here. The first is the problem of communication. It was essential for the supreme governing

[1] Bruns, *Fontes*[7], 28, 130.

body in the State, the Senate, to have first-hand information of the condition of the provinces and the political alignments of foreign powers. It was equally necessary to be in direct communication with allied and independent princes. Hence there arose a highly developed system of embassies. On the one hand the Senate would give plenipotentiary powers to one or more of its members to act in its name where a decision had to be taken overseas; on the other, it encouraged the provinces and the kings alike to send envoys to Rome to put their case directly before the Senate.

### EMBASSIES FROM ROME

The dignity and prestige of the Roman ambassador were carefully upheld. Cicero attributed a special sacrosanctity to the rights of *legatio*,[1] and he represents an ambassador, Popilius, as bearing in himself 'the image of the Senate and the authority of the Roman People'.[2] An ambassador had no *imperium*, but his *auctoritas* was sufficient to give him great influence; in 60 the Senate sent ambassadors 'with authority' to see that the states of Gaul did not make common cause with the Helvetii. Failure to respect the privileges of a Roman ambassador could not be condoned, as the Veneti found to their cost in 56.

For the appointment of the ambassadors a decree of the Senate was necessary which laid down the number and qualifications of the embassy; the personnel was appointed by the presiding magistrate in accordance with the Senate's directions. Both methods, of lot and election, are found in use; the ambassadors to Gaul in 60

[1] *de harus.* 16, 34.    [2] *Phil.* VIII, 8, 23.

were chosen by lot, but Appian mentions that the Senate had definitely directed the consul himself to choose and send ambassadors to Attalus.[1]

On appointment the ambassador received a generous equipment.[2] Clodius' meanness towards Cato in granting him only two clerks for his mission to Cyprus was a studied insult. As long as his office lasted he received a *viaticum* paid in the form of a daily allowance. He also had the traditional right of making demands upon public and private hospitality.[3] On an ordinary embassy (unlike a 'free' embassy) there was no time-limit; and there was nothing to prevent an envoy from travelling to his destination by a circuitous route. Cicero is indignant at Vatinius' meanderings through Sardinia and Africa, but he cannot brand them as definitely illegal.[4]

Embassies were despatched from Rome for various purposes. Some embassies were formal missions to convey congratulations and greetings to friendly princes. In 59 Clodius was chosen as an envoy to bear the good wishes of the Roman people to Tigranes, on entering upon his new kingdoms of Gordyene and Sophene. Such embassies offered little scope for private enrichment— Cicero calls this the 'bare task of a dispatch-runner'[5]— and we do not find that Clodius ever took up the commission. If the mission was of a less formal nature there was more competition for the appointment. We have seen how many senators coveted the 'good fat job' (*ib.*) of settling the affairs of Egypt. A flagrant case of graft occurred in 89, when an embassy headed by M'. Aquilius

[1] App. *Mithr.* 6.
[2] *II in Verr.* v, 32, 83.
[3] *Phil.* ix, 3, 6.
[4] *in Vat.* 5, 12.
[5] *ad Att.* ii, 7, 2.

was sent to restore Nicomedes of Bithynia. The extravagant reward he demanded in return led the king to make an unprovoked attack on Mithridates in the hope of raising the necessary funds; and hence arose the Mithridatic War. Aquilius' dramatic punishment must have seemed highly appropriate to the oriental mind.

The Senate was not however blind to the possibilities of abuse latent in the office. It showed its disapproval of Aquilius' behaviour by abrogating all his acts. The *Lex Julia* definitely prohibited an ambassador from receiving money in the discharge of his duty, and this law seems to have been generally obeyed. Nor must we take isolated examples of corruption as typical; most embassies from Rome were straightforward and practical undertakings, in which ulterior motives played little or no part. The Sicilian Commission of 72 furnishes an example of the system at its best. In 75 the Senate had altered the local system of farming out the taxes. As a result of complaints a commission was appointed 'of the most respectable men' with full authority. After investigation on the spot, it resolved to maintain the *Lex Hieronica* in its entirety. Individual ambassadors too provide instances of the old incorruptibility. Appius Claudius, when sent by Lucullus on a mission to Tigranes, refused all gifts but one small cup.[1] Jolliffe[2] says that he and Lucullus 'dare not compromise the government by trafficking with a potential enemy'; but we need not reject a higher motive. We remember that when Lucullus himself visited Egypt in 81 to collect a fleet for Sulla he too politely declined the gifts which were lavished on him.

[1] Plut. *Luc.* 21.    [2] *Op. cit.* p. 97.

Two particular forms of embassy deserve brief mention. On the acquisition of new territory a special commission was sent out to assist the general to fix the boundaries, and to draw up the *Lex provinciae*. Perhaps in theory this was merely appointed to convey the Senate's authority to the general, but in practice it would be largely responsible for the actual decision. Sometimes, in fact, the Senate gave definite instructions to the envoys as to the line of conduct to follow.[1]

Usually these commissions consisted of ten members, but only four others followed Scipio Nasica to Asia in 132. In 129 the full complement was sent out to help in the formal organisation of the new province of Asia. Among its decisions was one by which Phrygia was handed over to the king of Pontus. The fact that the revocation of this grant was commonly admitted to be a discreditable chapter of Roman diplomacy proves that the commission had acted with full authority in its arrangements.[2] A similar commission of ten helped Rupilius to organise Sicily in 131; Cicero avers that Verres was the first governor to neglect the settlement it had made. In 67 the news of Lucullus' victories led the Senate to suppose that the East was ripe for settlement, and a commission of ten was sent out, which included, contrary to usual custom, the general's brother, and his friend Murena.[3]

Pompey apparently carried out his settlement of Asia Minor without any such assistance, relying on the

[1] This appears from Livy's account of the commission sent to help Paulus in the organisation of Macedonia; Livy, XLV, 18.

[2] The status of Phrygia became a party question at Rome: the bill to confirm the grant was opposed by C. Gracchus (*v. supra*, p. 48).

[3] *ad Att.* XIII, 6, 4.

authority of the *Lex Manilia,* nor do we hear of the
Senate playing any part in the organisation of Gaul. It
is uncertain whether the decisions of a general and a
commission, working together, needed a formal decree
of the Senate to ratify them, but it does seem that where
a general acted alone, this senatorial confirmation was
indispensable. The Senate offended Pompey by refusing
to confirm his *acta en bloc,* while Cicero stated in 55 that
Caesar's victories would need legal ratification.[1]

The 'free embassy' was intended originally as a
method of overcoming the regulation which forbade a
senator to leave Italy. Its holder had no official duties,
but enjoyed all the privileges of an ambassador. The
institution was flatly condemned by Cicero, who declared that 'nothing is more disgraceful than that the
rights of legation should be granted for private ends';
yet he himself was not above asking Cornificius to
bestow on such legates the same privileges as he had
done in Cilicia.[2]

The *Ius Legationis Liberae* was restricted to senators.
Its holder was sacrosanct, and had the right to free en-
tertainment and lodging. Cicero belittles his authority
in speaking on the agrarian laws, but merely to heighten
by contrast the power of the proposed decemvirs. In
practice such a legate was powerful enough to be a
nuisance to the governor, and a burden to the provincials.
He was responsible to no one for his behaviour, and the
field of his action was unlimited.

The Senate did make some attempt to prevent too
flagrant a misuse of the privilege. In 63 Cicero as consul
proposed with the full support of the Senate to abolish

[1] *de prov. cons.* 8, 19.          [2] *ad fam.* XII, 21.

the system completely. The veto of a tribune prevented
the measure from becoming law, but the good faith of
the Senate is shown by the fact that Cicero actually succeeded in limiting the term of such embassies to one
year. Caesar incorporated this regulation in his own
legislation; there is no need to accept Arnold's contention that he increased the limit to five years.[1] The Julian
Law also limited the legal requisitions, and prohibited
the extension of the legate's privileges to the personal
friends of the governor. Piso apparently defied this
law by issuing the necessary *diplomata* to all and sundry.[2]

Usually senators obtained these appointments in order
to transact their private business in the provinces, but
political motives too may often be traced. The institution served as a pretext for the voluntary withdrawal or
the benevolent banishment of a senator from Italy.
Cicero twice dallied with the idea of avoiding the attacks
of his enemies in this way, in 59 and again in 44. In 55
the Triumvirs wanted to rid Rome of Clodius and arranged a *libera legatio* for him; but perhaps the plan fell
through, as we hear of him being present in Rome the
following year.

On the whole these roving commissions were frankly
an abuse. Meyer styles the institution 'eine der
schlimmsten Geiszeln der Provinzialen'.[3] But it does
show the respect which the Romans paid to the authority
of the *legatus* and the value they set upon his rights and
privileges.

[1] *Op. cit.* p. 85; his assumption depends on the mention of *quinquennium* in *ad Att.* xv, 11, 4.                              [2] *in Pis.* 37, 90.
[3] Meyer, *Caesars Monarchie*, p. 77.

### EMBASSIES TO ROME

Arnold dismisses the provincial embassies to Rome as of little consequence, but often they served a very useful purpose. Just as foreign states had no permanent legations in Rome, so the provinces had no High Commissioners to represent them. It was only by temporary embassies that they could bring themselves to the notice of Rome.

The Senate had early established its right to receive envoys from the foreign princes and the provinces. The only limitation imposed was that the envoys of an enemy power should not be received within the walls, and that no king should be allowed to visit Rome in person. At first the embassies were received as soon as possible after the entry of the new consuls into office, and if an embassy arrived later in the year its reception was often postponed *ad novos consules*; this was the regular custom by the time of Verres.[1] It was formulated by the *Lex Pupia* and confirmed in 67 by a *Lex Gabinia* which gave foreign embassies precedence in the month of February each year. No other business could be transacted in this month until all the embassies in Rome had been given a hearing.[2] Lange and Mommsen think that the object of the law was to lessen the opportunities for corruption by shortening the stay of the embassies in Rome, but it was probably introduced mainly in the interests of efficient administration; for it was naturally of advantage to have full information about the state of the provinces before allotting them to the magistrates. It was further

---

[1] *II in Verr.* ii, 31, 76.     [2] *ad Q.F.* ii, 11 (13), 3.

enacted that the Senate's answer should be handed over
to the embassy within ten days of their audience.

This arrangement was not entirely proof against inefficiency. The Senate could always postpone the hearing
of the embassies, even if this meant holding up all other
business until March. In 61 the Senate refused to receive
the embassies until the composition of the court to try
Clodius had been settled, while in 57 Cicero took it as a
personal compliment that all audiences were postponed
until after his recall. In the following year they were
certainly put off until February 13, and Cicero mentions
the possibility of their not being granted at all.[1] The
two sons of King Antiochus, who laid claim to the throne
of Egypt, were put off two years in succession in this
way. The arrangement of the agenda rested with the
consuls, and their decision was purely arbitrary. Much
depended on the order and manner of an embassy's introduction. Cicero graphically describes the Milesian
envoys who were eagerly awaiting the result of the
election, to know whether their complaints about Verres
would stand the chance of a favourable hearing. If the
consul bore the embassy ill-will, he could either put it
at the end of the list or introduce it in the rôle of devil's
advocate.

The influence of the consuls opened the door wide to
corruption, but the practice of demanding money from
the embassies was condemned by all responsible opinion
at Rome. In 94 the Senate had ordained that no money
should be loaned to foreign envoys while they were in
the capital; this was a sensible attempt to cut off the
source of bribery. The decree was re-enacted in 70 with

[1] *ad Att.* i, 14, 5; *ad Q.F.* ii, 3, 1; *ad fam.* i, 4, 1.

especial reference to the Cretans, who were obviously hoping to buy support on a large scale.[1] In 67 Cornelius tried to make this a general enactment. The Senate approved of the principle but disliked the sponsor of the law; it may well have been justified in its contention that its recent decree did everything that could be done by legislation. Cornelius' 'importunity' failed;[2] but his colleague Gabinius later succeeded in incorporating the proposed regulation into a law which he passed through the Assembly. By this, any money lent to the ambassadors was not recoverable at law.[3] Long[4] thinks that the object of the law was to prevent the efflux of precious metals from Italy, but this is unnecessary. Nor is Jolliffe justified in saying that 'the Senate made every effort to circumvent the law'. The dispensation granted to the noble Brutus was the exception which proved that the rule was usually maintained. It is as well to remember too for the sake of proportion that the majority of the embassies were concerned with routine business and offered little scope for large-scale corruption.

Usually the envoys returned home as soon as they had finished their business, but until they had left the city they had the powers of a permanent legation. An embassy of the Macedonians, present in another connection, gave evidence on behalf of Plancius' good behaviour in that province. The envoys of Deiotarus were in Rome for at least a year about 45, and sent the king frequent reports on the state of affairs at Rome. In the same year

---

[1] Jolliffe (*op. cit.* p. 103) strangely makes the first decree also refer to the Cretans alone.

Asc. *in Corn.* 57.　　　　　　　[3] *ad Att.* v, 21, 12.
*Ciceronis Orationes*, p. 269.

(45) envoys from Cnidus were compelled to wait until autumn before completing their business, owing to the absence of Caesar in Spain.[1] Such long stays were not, however, encouraged by the Senate; it seems never to have realised the advantages of having a representative of a province or king permanently resident in the capital. In case of need it preferred to send an especial summons for an *ad hoc* embassy to come to Rome. When for instance the rumour arrived that the province of Asia was in sympathy with Mithridates, a certain Xenocles was summoned from Adramyttene to give an explanation.[2]

The business of these embassies was of many kinds. The states of Sicily sent envoys to ask for help against Verres. Oropus and Adramyttene appealed against the extortion of the *publicani*. In 51 Mylasa complained about its debts to a private citizen, Cluvius; apparently in this case the embassy had no plenipotentiary powers to negotiate, but could only report to the home government.[3] When Q. Cicero referred the customs question to the Senate, envoys were sent to represent the provincial interests. The personnel of the embassies was equally various. Naturally they were composed of responsible members of the city or nation, men of some weight. Antiochus sent his two sons to Rome; it was the 'leaders of the Macedonian states' who spoke for Plancius. In 61 an embassy of druids, under Diviciacus, sent by the Aedui, attracted attention at Rome.[4] The Alexandrians sent no less than 100 ambassadors, under

---

[1] See C. Cichorius, 'Ein Bundnisvertrag zwischen Rom und Knidos', *Rhein. Mus.* LXXVI, 1927, p. 327.

[2] Strabo, XIII, 614.          [3] *ad fam.* XIII, 56, 1.

[4] *de div.* I, 41, 90.

the leadership of the academician Dion, to discuss the restoration of Ptolemy.

The practice of sending embassies to Rome became so popular that the governors found it necessary to discourage it in the interests of economy. We know of at least five embassies arriving in one year, 54. Envoys from Tenedos appealed for their autonomy. Magnesia sent a deputation in honour of Q. Cicero. A taxation-dispute led to counter-embassies of the Tyrians and the Syrian tax-gatherers; a delegate of Antiochus of Commagene was busy ingratiating himself with the consul Appius. The 'crowded Senate' accorded to the Tyrians is an instance of the interest taken in these embassies.

Little practical purpose was served by one kind of embassy. The *encomia* sent after a retiring governor may have once been genuine and deserved expressions of personal gratitude, but they had become a mere form. Sulla tried to limit them by cutting down the expenses which might be incurred in their despatch, but it was impossible to suppress them. The situation became farcical when envoys arrived from Syracuse in honour of Verres at the very time that the dossier was being prepared for his prosecution; however, as Cicero hints,[1] the Senate took very little notice of such embassies.

The second great difficulty which the Senate had to face was the problem of defence. The question was complicated by the fact that the empire had not yet reached a natural frontier,[2] and that the military system was devised for the city-state rather than for a world-power; but the Senate always recognised, if it sometimes failed to fulfil, its task of imperial defence.

[1] *ad fam.* III, 8, 3.          [2] Cf. *in Pis.* 16, 38.

'It was the first duty of the Roman governor to protect his province from without',[1] and most governors
were fully alive to their responsibilities. Cicero, despite
his yearning for Rome, was determined to stay on in
Cilicia as long as the safety of the country demanded his
presence. In the midst of his activity in Gaul, Caesar
found time to protect the frontier of Illyricum against
the Pirustae. Successive generals conducted campaigns
from Macedonia against the Thracians. In neglecting
the safety of their provinces Piso and Gabinius showed
themselves notable exceptions to the general rule.[2]

Rome could rely on two ancillary supports in her
efforts. The one was the resources of the client-kingdoms, the other was constituted by the Roman settlements which were established at strategic points. Cicero
referred to the military colony at Narbo Martius as a
'watch-tower and bulwark of the Roman people',[3] while
the settlements in Spain were commonly called 'garri-
sons'.[4] The main responsibility however rested on the
armed forces of the Roman government.

[1] Arnold, *op. cit.* p. 43.

[2] *ad Att.* VI, 6, 3; Caesar, *b.g.* v, 1; *pro Font.* 20, 44.

[3] *pro Font.* 1, 13.

[4] τὰ φρούρια: App. *Hisp.* 38. It is probable that these settlements
did not receive the formal title of 'colony' until the time of Caesar, but
the name was sometimes loosely applied to them; for instance, Livy
(XLIII, 3) refers to Carteia as *colonia civium Latinorum et libertinorum* in
171 (see Pauly-Wissowa, *Colonia, Carteia*). If, however, Carteia really
was a colony at this date, it was, with Narbo Martius, the only example
of a successful transmarine colony in the time of the Republic.

### THE ARMY

The old citizen militia of the Roman People had long become a myth. After the reforms of Marius the army was a professional body. Henceforth the soldier enlisted for the duration of his active life, and we rarely find the time-expired veteran pressing for his discharge. His release was, as Last points out,[1] an issue that was only raised by the political enemies of the general concerned. Since there was no state pension to be expected, he was only willing to be demobilised if his general could offer him good prospects of a gratuity or a small-holding. The discontent under Lucullus was due to his hard discipline and the machinations of Clodius, for even the old campaigners of Flaccus and Fimbria promptly signed on again for service under Pompey. Similarly the 'grievances' of Caesar's troops in 51 were exploited by his opponents. They succeeded in getting a decree passed that any soldier who wished for his discharge should apply to the Senate, but we do not hear of any mass-movement to take advantage of this privilege.

The Senate did not, however, make full use of the new professional organisation of the army. Instead it tried to fit it in to the old system by which the army only came into being for the campaign. This meant on the one hand vast armies of 'unposted' veterans, dependent on their general and ready for mischief, and on the other a shortage of troops on the spot to deal with any emergency in the province.

[1] *C.A.H.* ix, 136.

Even if we allow for the great 'private armies' of Caesar and Pompey, the strength of the Roman forces was admittedly unequal to the duties which they had to perform. The Senate had a rooted mistrust of committing too large an army to the command of one man, while the difficulty of obtaining recruits became more and more pressing. In 55 Pompey and Crassus resorted to conscription, but this example does not seem to have been followed. What forces there were in a province were concentrated on the frontier. Peaceful provinces were almost denuded. Mithridates' triumphal advance over Asia in 88 met with little opposition, for not one of the five hundred towns in the province had a Roman garrison. Similarly, Sertorius' initial successes in Spain were due to the absence of any proper Roman army.

After the appointment of the governor it rested with the Senate to decide what troops he should be allowed. Except in the case of the extraordinary commands, there were rarely more than two legions to any one province. There was only one Roman legion in Asia in 88. Cicero was, to his great disappointment, only granted two legions in Cilicia in 51; 'such a puny troop compared with Caesar's brigades!'[1] After the pacification of Macedonia, Cicero assures us that it was held by little more than the moral force of the governor.[2] In times of emergency the Senate increased its grant. It added an extra legion to Caesar's army in 59, and allowed him to enrol two more on his own responsibility in Cisalpine Gaul in 57. In 55 it gave Pompey and Crassus *carte blanche* to enrol up to seven legions each. The unrest in Spain under Nepos in the previous year was largely due

[1] *ad Att.* v, 15, 1.          [2] *de prov. cons.* 3, 5.

to the weakness of the garrison,[1] and the Senate may have determined to extinguish the last smouldering embers of revolt. In 51 the situation in the East led the Senate to post two extra legions thither, under the leadership of Bibulus' quaestor Marius.

Sometimes, too, a governor was able to make use of troops who were already in the province. When Lucullus sailed for Asia in 74 the Senate could only afford to grant him one fresh legion, but this was merely a small part of the forces at his disposal. The province itself was still garrisoned by the two legions which had originally been brought out by the ill-fated consul of 86, L. Valerius Flaccus; on his death they had been taken over by his brutal successor C. Flavius Fimbria. They were hard-bitten old veterans who had slain one general and betrayed another. Yet their training and experience made them a first-rate fighting force, if only they were strongly handled, and Lucullus soon won their respect, if not their personal loyalty. There were, moreover, two other legions at his disposal. These were the soldiers taken out to Cilicia by P. Servilius Isauricus in 78, and they were of a much better type. They had seen hard service in the mountains of Isauria, but they had not yet been in the East long enough to lose their Roman traditions or be corrupted by oriental luxury. Hence his forces would amount in all to five legions of 6000 men each; but the total of effectives would be far less than the 30,000 mentioned by Plutarch. He had also a body of cavalry variously estimated at 1600 and 2500.[2] His

---

[1] Cf. Dio, xxxvii, 52; Caesar is compelled in 61 to increase his army from twenty to thirty cohorts.

[2] The lower figure is Appian's, the higher Plutarch's.

army was of course vastly outnumbered by the forces of Mithridates, and but for Lucullus' military genius, the cautious parsimony of the Senate might well have led to disaster.

The Senate also controlled the recruitment and pay of the legions. Before Cicero could hold a levy it was necessary for a *senatus consultum* to be passed. This was blocked by the consul Sulpicius but eventually carried. Besides its initial grant of money, the Senate forwarded a sum for the payment of the troops each year that a governor's command was prolonged. At the rate of 600,000 denarii a legion this was a severe strain on the Treasury; but, to give the Senate its due, it did not grudge opening its purse-strings if it was convinced that the need was justified. Pompey's urgent demand note from Spain in 74 was promptly met, while in 55 Cicero himself proposed that the Senate should take over financial responsibility for Caesar's two new legions. This was despite the fact that the booty from the Gauls would probably have covered the cost, and that the Treasury was passing through a very difficult period. Nor was the Senate unbusinesslike in its methods. When the question of Pompey's stipend arose in 51, pert enquiries were made as to the status of the legion lent to Caesar; and the draft was not passed until this had been explained.[1]

The Senate erred in not abandoning its out-of-date conception of the Roman army as a citizen militia; but the real weakness of the Roman military system lay in the failure to make use of 'the excellent material provided by the provinces'[2] themselves. Provision was

[1] *ad fam.* VIII, 4, 4.          [2] Stevenson, *C.A.H.* IX, 449.

made for the employment of native auxiliaries but little
reliance was placed on them as a rule. Lucullus, whose
cavalry was hopelessly inadequate to cope with Mithridates' strong mounted arm, made little attempt to
strengthen it with native levies. Deiotarus had a very
capable force of Galatian cavalry which did good service
in the early days of the war and later accompanied the
Roman army to Tigranocerta; there was also a troop
of Thracian horsemen attached to the Asiatic legions.
But on the whole these auxiliaries were employed rather
as scouts and skirmishers than as an integral part of the
army. Cicero wrote to the Senate that to recruit and
train provincials was as dangerous as it was wasteful.[1]
He himself made no requisition for the Transpadane
cavalry which belonged to him by right; Bibulus refused
to conduct levies at all in Syria.

Cicero admitted that the auxiliaries of Galatia,
Pisidia and Lycia formed the backbone of his army,[2] but
these were troops taken over *en bloc* from semi-inde-
pendent communities. The system of incorporating
native troops under Roman officers, as a part of the
Roman army proper, was almost unknown. It was left
for Caesar to reveal the possibilities of the provincial
as a Roman soldier. The continual inroads of the
Thracians were largely due to the fact that the Macedonians had been disarmed and were unable to help in
their own defence. Perhaps the Senate feared to put
arms into the hands of its subjects; but the fact that a
province could be so denuded of troops seems to show
that there was no such widespread discontent with
Roman rule as to justify such a precaution.

[1] *ad fam.* xv, 1, 5.                    [2] *ad Att.* vi, 5, 3.

## THE NAVY

Rome was not a naval power, and the policing of the seas was usually left to the provincial governors. The increasing menace of the pirates led to the special naval commands of Antonius and Pompeius, but it was only gradually realised that a strong and permanent fleet was essential for the well-being of the empire. In 86 Lucullus had taken two years to collect a fleet to act against Mithridates. In the Third Mithridatic War it was not until the Pontic ships had been damaged by storm in 71 that the Roman fleet was able to enter the Black Sea. But the Senate was not blind to the moral. No less a sum than 18 million sesterces was offered to Lucullus for the purpose of equipping a fleet, and after Pompey had brought his operations to a close it was resolved to keep the fleet in commission. In 62 the Senate went further, and at Pompey's suggestion established a permanent fleet in Italian waters, a sum of 4,300,000 sesterces being voted for the purpose.[1] A further grant was passed in 61, and the fleet probably remained in being until the Civil War.

Before the establishment of the imperial fleets, Rome had depended on local squadrons, built, equipped and for the most part manned by provincials. A governor could collect a fleet either by laying the provision of one or more ships on a community as a special impost, or by paying for it from the proceeds of a particular tax. In 63 a decree of the Senate authorised the collection of 'ship-money' in Asia, but this was merely the repetition of earlier decrees with the same import. The total

[1] *pro Flacc.* 13, 30.

amount of the tax to be collected, as also the assessment of the various communities, was left to the discretion of the governor, nor had he to render accounts for its disposal. Hence there was ample opportunity for malversation. Jolliffe estimates that Verres' total gains from naval administration were at least £10,000 a year. There were other governors who emulated if they did not equal his peculations, for Cicero mentions the abuse in 66.[1] Later he had to defend Flaccus, an ex-governor of Asia, who was explicitly charged with such embezzlement. He had a difficult task, for Flaccus could only point to two small coasting squadrons as the visible result of a heavy imposition of ship-money. We may note that his successor, Q. Cicero, did not impose a tax at all. Perhaps, however, he kept part of the large fleet left by Pompey on a 'care and maintenance' basis, ready for use in case of emergency.

It does not seem however that the payment of ship-money proved very burdensome to the provincials as a rule. It has always been a particularly unpopular tax, but except in the cases mentioned we rarely hear of specific complaints. There is no ground for supposing that the fleet Lucullus collected from the allies was unnecessarily large, while the ten ships demanded by Murena from Miletus could easily be supplied by such a wealthy city.[2] Nor was Pompey's vast fleet due to megalomania, for it was amply justified by the result of its ⟨activities. The communities were quite willing to insure themselves against the depredations of the pirates by contributions of ships or money; and few governors would extend their malversation beyond the petty ap-

---

[1] *de imp. Cn. Pomp.* 23, 67.    [2] *II in Verr.* 1, 35, 89.

propriation of any surplus funds or stores. The system of local control was inferior to the situation; but the Senate itself finally recognised this, and by its establishment of a permanent squadron off the Italian coast, it took an important step towards that freedom of the seas of which Horace sings: *pacatum volitant per mare navitae.*

## CHAPTER VI

## ROMAN RULE IN PRACTICE

W<small>E</small> have discussed in the preceding chapter the part played by the Senate in the administration of the provinces. Let us in conclusion consider briefly the effects of Roman rule from the point of view of the provincial himself. In doing so two facts must be remembered. The first is that it is dangerously easy to judge in the light of our own experiences, and by our own moral standards, and the second is that our main evidence, the speeches of Cicero, concentrates rather upon the seamy side of the picture. When he speaks on behalf of a provincial governor he is usually making the best of a bad case; while those whom he attacks were by no means representative specimens.[1]

Admittedly, the system had its weak points. There was no Civil Service, and hence the institution of tax-farming, with its attendant evils, was inevitable. Despite tentative efforts in the right direction the Senate never completely abandoned the system of short commands. Frequent replacement of the governor led to a lack of continuity in administration, and increased the rapacity of a governor who wanted to get rich quickly. It added also to the difficulty of frontier defence, for the governor had often no local knowledge of the problems at issue.

[1] Verres was condemned by all responsible and unbiased opinion at Rome. Piso had already shown his lack of principle during his consulate by his connivance at Clodius' irregularities.

By uniting all the departments of State in one man, the Senate paid a not undeserved compliment to the versatility of its members, but it could scarcely expect them to carry out all their functions with the same skill. The wide powers enjoyed by the governor made some permanent court of appeal in Rome more than ever essential; the absence of this did much to hinder the Senate's control over the governors. The military system was unsatisfactory, and left the soldiers too dependent on the general, while all the efforts of legislators did not succeed in adjusting the relations between governor and Treasury on a basis that would be proof against malversation.

Greenidge points to a fundamental inconsistency of ideas in the Roman system; in his opinion the theory aimed at 'the impossible combination of martial law with municipal independence'. This is as dangerous as so many half-truths. The amount of autonomy left to the natives was one of the strongest points in the system. What would now be called 'martial law' was then the only attitude open to a conquering power. But it is true that the Romans often tolerated inefficiency in the municipalities and allowed the native officials too free a hand. Cicero was astonished at the peculations of the Greek magistrates in Cilicia. It is equally true that little or no effort was made to take the native into partnership as an equal. The Romans were jealous of their privileges. There was a prejudice against the possession by provincial cities of the status of *colonia* or *municipium*. Wholesale extensions of the franchise were viewed with disfavour, and its grant to individuals was regarded as a rare concession. Usually it was given as

a reward for distinguished military service, and gradually
the custom became established that a victorious general
had the right to bestow the franchise upon his soldiers.[1]
As a rule, such an extraordinary grant was confirmed by
a special law: this tended to become a mere form towards the end of the period, but it remained necessary
in theory. By his wholesale enfranchisement of a troop
of Spanish cavalry in 89 Cn. Pompeius Strabo showed
himself surprisingly free from the narrow prejudice with
which the Romans viewed the franchise question. His
example was not followed on a large scale until the end
of the Republic.[2]

## EXTORTION

The administration of the provinces largely depended
on the governor, despite the checks on his action. He
was undoubtedly exposed to great temptations; a province was in fact the recognised way of recouping one's
losses at Rome. Cicero declares that unless Piso had
obtained a good province he could not have remained
solvent. He himself could deposit 2,200,000 sesterces
at Ephesus before leaving Asia without incurring a
breath of suspicion. A rascal like Piso 'extorted large
sums from Dyrrhachium, despoiled the Thessalians,
imposed fixed annual contributions on the Achaeans'.[3]
Gabinius made £4,000,000 out of his tenure of office
in Syria; and yet Josephus can praise his rule as being

[1] *pro Balbo*, 23, 53; see Arnold, *op. cit.* p. 73.

[2] See article by Stevenson, 'Cn. Pompeius Strabo and the Franchise
Question', *J.R.S.* IX, 1919, p. 95; also Cichorius, *Römische Studien*,
p. 130 (Berlin, 1922).

    *ad fam.* v, 20, 9; *pro Sest.* 43, 94; and see Jolliffe, *op. cit., passim.*

on the whole equitable.[1] Rich communities earmarked a special 'praetor's fund' to meet any extraordinary requisitions from the governor.[2] The governor was not confined to direct demands for money. By extravagant progresses through the countryside he could lay bare his province. The billeting of troops provided him with a subtle means of wringing money out of reluctant communities. The Cyprians paid two hundred talents a year for exemption from this burden.[3]

If Arnold exaggerates when he says that 'there was little or no idea that Rome had duties to the provincials as well as rights',[4] it is true that there was a strong body of opinion which regarded the provinces as fields for plunder. A governor's friends at Rome all expected their share of his gains. The aediles took it as a matter of course that the provinces should help to pay for their games; this contribution was regularly styled *aedilicium vectigal*. Cicero, despite his assertion that Asia was the only province which did more than pay for the expenses of administration, admits in writing to the Senate that the provinces provide the income of the Roman People. He stresses the financial stake in the Mithridatic War, while Dio praises Pompey for having provided the State with so many fresh sources of income. The same author tells us that Lucullus refused the province of Sardinia because of the evil repute attached to the very name of governor.[5]

The harm a governor wrought could extend to the

[1] Dio, xxxix, 55; Jos. *Ant.* xiv, 5, 2.

[2] *ad Att.* v, 21, 11.        [3] *Ibid.*

[4] *Op. cit.* p. 81.

[5] *ad Q.F.* i, 1, 26; *de imp. Cn. Pomp.* 6, 14; *ad fam.* xv, 1, 5; Dio, xxxvii, 20; *ib.* xxxvi, 39.

person as well as the pocket. Three names stand out as
examples of misgovernment. Verres and Piso were
directly pilloried by Cicero, Appius was his predecessor
in Cilicia, and figures largely in his correspondence.
Verres inaugurated his career well by reversing the
wrong decisions of his quaestor and by checking the
activities of the tax-collectors, but he soon showed his
true colours by acting in collusion with them. He neglected local privileges by requisitioning a ship from
Tauromenium; he allowed the army to disintegrate,
and entrusted the chief command in the navy to an unqualified Sicilian. He obtained money by selling local
offices, and by making demands for statues and thank-
offerings. Instead of administering justice on circuit, he
stayed in Syracuse and held court there, altering his
edict at will. As a result of his oppression the whole
people lost hope to such an extent that it ceased to
cultivate the fields; a method of silent protest which is
believed to exist in Russia to-day.

Piso was a governor of similar calibre. He roused a
mutiny by not paying his troops, and openly sold promotion in the army. On leaving the province he demobilised his forces; Cicero suggests that he had previously encouraged the aggressions of the Thracians.
He used his position to establish a 'corner' in leather.
He over-rode the rights of the free peoples, and acted
with treachery towards friendly chieftains. Finally, we
are told that he did his best to impede the lawful activities of the tax-farmers; but as Cicero regards Piso from
a frankly partisan standpoint, this may merely mean that
he objected to the provincials being plucked by other
hands than his own.

The evidence against Appius is less cumulative, but
more effective because in giving it Cicero is not stating
a case. For political reasons he dared not break with
Appius. He testified to his high character when he was
accused of extortion, and he writes to him with restrained politeness; but he allows his real feelings to
come out in his private letters to Atticus. Apparently
Appius had thoroughly disorganised the army, so that
Cicero could find no trace of three whole cohorts. He
deliberately insulted Cicero on the latter's arrival; when
he departed, he left letters with his legates complaining
of Cicero's behaviour to himself! As an example of his
misgovernment may be cited his ready grant of a prefecture and a troop of cavalry to Scaptius the moneylender,[1] to enable him to terrorise the Salaminians into
submission. Cicero roundly declares that he had behaved in the province like a wild beast, and that the
whole country was one gaping wound to be healed.[2]

It is dangerous, however, to generalise too confidently
from the examples of these three governors. Cicero

[1] The affair of Scaptius is narrated in detail by Cicero in a letter to
Atticus (ad Att. v, 21, 10). Apparently he was the financial agent of the
noble Brutus; with the help afforded by Appius he was attempting to
recover £50,000 from the people of Salamis, this sum representing the
principal and interest at 48 per cent. on a loan made by Brutus and his
friends. Brutus had even induced the Senate to pass a special decree
dispensing the transaction from the law of Gabinius which forbade lending
to provincials. Cicero did his best to protect the Salaminians from their
creditors, and to arrange a compromise, at the risk of a quarrel with
Brutus; and he himself refused to confirm Scaptius' prefecture. 'I in-
formed him I always refused business men. So I have already told you.'
This unsavoury episode shows the influence of the moneylender if he had
the support, or even the connivance, of the governor.

[2] ad Att. v, 16, 2.

more than once utters a sweeping condemnation of the system as a whole,[1] but even when he is not openly speaking to a brief, it is easy to find an ulterior motive. Either he is wishing to extol his hero Pompey, by contrast, or to stress the mildness of his own rule, 'which seemed almost incredible'.[2] Roman rule was, indeed, unpopular in Asia,[3] but this seems to have been exceptional. The Asiatics were an effeminate race, and it is little wonder that the effete luxury of the province proved too much for some governors. In general, Rome might well claim that her direct and indirect impositions were merely the necessary payment for her protection. As Cicero says, 'That rule cannot in any way be upheld without taxes; so let the provincials pay some part of their income for unbroken peace with an easy mind.'[4]

Moreover, some if not most of the governors seem to have maintained a high standard of administration. Cicero states it as a truism that the first care of the governor is for those whom he governs.[5] That this was something more than the assertion of a mere ideal is shown by the undoubted popularity of many of the governors. The memory of Scaevola was kept green by a festival in his honour at Smyrna. In 50 Cicero singles out Thermus of Asia, Silius of Bithynia, and Nonius of Crete and Cyrene for special praise.[6] As quaestor in

[1] E.g., *II in Verr.* III, 89, 207; *de imp. Cn. Pomp.* 22, 64; *ad fam.* xv, 1, 5: *acerbitatem atque iniurias imperii nostri.*

[2] *ad Att.* v, 18, 2.

[3] Memnon (38) tells us that the tax-gatherers were so unpopular in Asia that they were murdered on their arrival at Heraclea.

[4] *ad Q.F.* I, 1, 34.

[5] *ad Q.F.* I, 1, 24.

[6] *ad Att.* VI, 1, 13.

Macedonia, Sestius was remembered for many years. Verres' abolition of the festival in honour of Marcellus at Syracuse was received with indignation by the province. Cicero mentions the scrupulous care with which L. Piso, as propraetor in Spain, avoided all suspicion of dishonesty in his dealings with the natives. Many of the governors were as poor when leaving a province as on entry. P. Lentulus Spinther had to sell his estates shortly after his return from Cilicia; Appius Claudius (senior) and Dolabella, governors of Macedonia and Asia respectively, both left their families in poverty.[1]

The numerous inscriptions extant in honour of Servilius Isauricus cannot all be due to sycophancy; Cicero tells him that the fame of his administration has reached Rome. The same authority stressed the self-control of Pompey, who behaved to the subject races as 'an angel from heaven'. The discovery of his secret financial interests may have tarnished his halo for Cicero, but his popularity in the East is shown by the support it gave him in the Civil War. Caesar, too, made enough money in Spain to pay off his debts, but he did much for the province. He persuaded the tribes to settle their disputes amicably, he induced the Senate to remit taxation, and he introduced a sound debt law. He paid special attention to the towns, enlarging and modernising Gades, and introducing Roman civilisation.[2]

More conservative proconsuls showed the same enlightenment. Cicero reveals the inner history of his term

---

[1] *pro Sest.* 5, 13; *II in Verr.* ii, 20, 50; iv, 25, 55; *ad Att.* vi, 1, 23; Varro, *r.r.* iii, 16; *II in Verr.* i, 30, 77.

[2] *ad fam.* xiii, 68; *de imp. Cn. Pomp.* 14, 41; *ad fam.* xiii, 56, 3; *pro Balb.* 19, 43.

of office in his letters and emerges with a heightened reputation. He set out for Cilicia with the highest intentions. He exacted no 'maintenance' en route, he attempted to limit the futile deputations in honour of Appius, and he embarked on a comprehensive programme of economy. It is true that he had at times to sacrifice the well-being of the provincials to the interests of the capitalists; and to humour Appius he withdrew from his uncompromising attitude towards the deputations. But although Tyrrell may dub him a 'moral dandy', he did succeed in effecting many reforms. He refused Caelius a *vectigal aedilicium*, and he dismissed the brutal Gavius. He did not allow temples or shrines in his honour, and would not accept 'billeting-money' or requisitions of any kind. On the whole he well deserves the high praise accorded him by Plutarch and Quintilian.

There was, too, a general interest in the sound administration of the provinces. The feeling against Verres in the Senate shows what was thought of a bad governor. The *Lex Julia de repetundis*, with 101 clauses, was in large part a repetition of existing statutes, but its comprehensive scope made it a charter for the provincials. It limited the honours to be decreed to a governor, and upheld the privileges of the free cities. It repeated the *Lex Cornelia de maiestate*, by which a governor might not leave his province. It narrowly defined the legal requisitions which might be made; it was even made illegal to purchase anything but the necessaries of life in one's province. Further sections dealt with the publication of accounts and proceedings in cases of extortion. Although this legislation was introduced by an op-

ponent of the Senate it was universally welcomed; and
Cicero always mentions it with approval and respect.

## LUCULLUS IN ASIA

An outstanding instance of courage and statesmanship
was provided by Lucullus when he overhauled the
financial system of Asia; his firm handling of the
capitalists and his consideration for the provincials deserve detailed discussion as representing senatorial
government at its best.

When Lucullus landed in Asia in 74 he found the
economic condition of the province had gone from bad
to worse. The demands of the Roman creditors and tax-
farmers, and the burden of the troops who were billeted
on the province, were oppressing the inhabitants beyond
measure. Many of them were only waiting their time
to raise the flag of revolt once again. Lucullus had not
the time to make those sweeping reforms which were
necessary, but he interviewed leading representatives
of the tax-farmers and capitalists and put the matter
plainly to them. Unless they moderated their demands
they would endanger the Roman dominion in the whole
of Asia Minor. The capitalists reluctantly agreed to
make some concessions; that this temporary relief was
appreciated is shown by the general loyalty of Asia to
Rome throughout the war.[1]

After three years' campaigning Lucullus returned to
the province to find that the state of affairs was again

[1] Rice Holmes (I, 404) disproves Mommsen's statement (*Röm.
Gesch.* III³, 57) that 'Lucullus had to spend time pacifying the province
(of Asia)'.

critical. The capitalists had forgotten his warning and
were once more draining the province dry. The root of
the trouble lay in the burden of debt which the province
had gradually accumulated. The cities, worn out by the
First Mithridatic War, had been hopelessly unable to
pay their share of the indemnity. In their poverty they
had accepted the specious offers of Roman moneylenders,
and had borrowed their money at exorbitant rates of
interest. As security, they had mortgaged theatres,
gymnasiums, temples and all other public property;
sometimes even private property had been pledged for
public loans. The province had already paid the 20,000
talents imposed by Sulla twice over, but the debt had
increased so rapidly with the compound interest that it
now amounted to six times that amount. Apart from
this indemnity debt the country had also to raise the
ordinary revenue each year, which was collected by
Roman tax-farmers; this, the *vectigal*, consisted of the
harbour-dues, the pasture rent, and the tithe of all the
produce. The demands of the tax-farmer would not in
themselves have been intolerable; but combined with
the exactions of the *negotiatores* they were rapidly forcing
Asia into universal bankruptcy.

Lucullus was no Catiline who hankered after *novae
tabulae*. He knew that a sweeping cancellation of all
debts would be as unjust to the creditors as the present
system was to the debtors. He had the good sense,
moreover, not to interfere with the tax-farming methods.
Probably the financial interests at Rome would have
been strong enough to resist any attempt to introduce
direct taxation, and in any case the province would still
have had to find almost as much for the Treasury. He

confined himself to what was in his power; his reforms fall under four heads:

1. He limited the legal rate of interest to 12 per cent. This seems high to us, but it was the usual rate at Rome. Money was always 'dear' in classical times; and the credit of Asia was so unsound that 48 per cent. had become no uncommon rate.[1]

2. He cancelled the demands for outstanding interest in so far as it exceeded the capital originally lent. This meant that from now on the creditors could recover the capital they had lent at most doubled. On debts that had been outstanding since 84, this represented a rate of only 7 per cent. simple interest, or 5 per cent. compound; hence this provision resulted in a considerable loss to the creditor, even under the new conditions.

3. He limited the amount which a creditor could demand each year from his debtor to 25 per cent. of the latter's income from his fields, plus an additional sum fixed in proportion to the 'rateable value' of his property in slaves and houses. Such at least seems to be the only interpretation of Plutarch and Appian; the former authority makes it clear that this measure imposed no new 'fixed tribute of 25 per cent. of the harvest', as has been suggested, but was of purely general application.

4. He ordained that the reckoning of compound interest should in future invalidate the whole claim. The system seems to have been universally mistrusted in classical times on moral grounds. At the prevailing

---

[1] Cicero later fixed the same limit in Cilicia. In 51 a decree of the Senate seems to have established it as the legal rate for all provinces, but the evidence (*ad Att.* v, 21, 13) is vague.

high rates, such a method of reckoning certainly meant that the principal was multiplied at an alarming speed.[1]

The relief afforded by these measures was instantaneous. In less than four years the province was free from debt and all lands that had been seized under distraint were restored to their original owners. It was no wonder that the grateful natives regarded Lucullus with 'real affection',[2] and overwhelmed him with their thanks. Other parts of the empire might well grudge the province such a governor.

It is interesting to note that when Caesar went to Farther Spain in 61 he found himself faced with a very similar problem; and in dealing with it he perhaps unconsciously adopted the same methods as Lucullus. He found, however, that he could increase the creditor's quota to two-thirds of the debtor's income without putting an insupportable burden upon the latter; this was probably due to the much lower standard of living in the western province.

But while the grateful provincials were instituting special festivals in honour of Lucullus, the Roman world of finance, unused to such treatment, was already beginning to work for his downfall. Behind it stood the Equestrian order, with its growing political influence, which henceforth regarded Lucullus with bitter hostility. It was his courageous reorganisation of the finances of Asia that set in motion the forces which were eventually to lead to his own recall.

---

[1] Compound interest was later forbidden throughout the whole empire by Justinian (*Cod.* IV, 32, 38).

[2] Plutarch, *Life of Lucullus*, § 20.

## ADVANTAGES OF THE PROVINCIALS

Few governors would be willing, like Lucullus, to jeopardise their own prospects in the interests of the provincials; yet on the whole the provinces undoubtedly benefited from the introduction of Roman rule. First and foremost, the Roman defence of the frontier gave security from external invasion and aggression. The Gauls were protected from the Germans, the Cilicians from the Parthians. Almost as important was the internal peace which came in the train of the Roman supremacy. Stevenson[1] asserts that 'even under the republic Rome was fairly successful in policing the provinces'. Cicero warns Asia that if the Roman troops were withdrawn it would experience the whole gamut of external war and domestic strife.[2] Arnold[3] suggests with some truth that Rome did not know how to deal with races that had a native civilisation and culture as advanced as its own; but it certainly had a talent for introducing the primary essentials of civilisation into a nation of barbarians. Brigandage was suppressed in Spain and Illyria.[4] Barbaric customs, such as human sacrifice, were abolished. Caesar released the mass of the Gauls from their condition of feudal slavery. The spread of Roman rule was accompanied by the growth of towns and the construction of roads. Pompey founded forty new towns in Asia Minor; Vienne, we are told,[5] grew from a squalid village into a wealthy city under the stimulating protection of Rome.

[1] *C.A.H.* IX, 461.    [2] *ad Q.F.* I, 1, 34.    [3] *Op. cit.* p. 6.
[4] Caesar, *bell. civ.* I, 85; *bell. Alex.* 42.
[5] Strabo, IV, 186.

Cicero addresses a panegyric to his brother Quintus which is worth quoting at length. As a comprehensive picture of the Perfect Governor it may be idealised, but it does point the contrast between the moderation of the praetor and the licence of the potentate whom he displaced:[1]

'I hear that under your rule the states have contracted no new debts; many of them have in fact been relieved of the burdens under which they have been groaning. You have re-established a number of cities which had fallen into decay, and almost into desolation, among them Samos and Halicarnassus, the noblest cities of Ionia and Caria respectively. There is no faction or discord in the towns. You have taken care that the states shall be administered by the better classes. The brigands of Mysia have been removed, and riots have been put down in many places. In establishing order throughout the province you have not merely pacified the highroads and the countryside, but also suppressed the pillaging of towns and shrines. No longer do insidious accusations minister to the avarice of the praetor, and attack the fame and fortune of the wealthy in their retirement. The expenses of administration and the tribute imposed on the states are borne with easy mind by all who live within their boundaries. Access to you is easy, and your ears are open to the complaints of all. No one is so poor and uninfluential as to be denied approach to you, even when you are off duty at home. In a word there is nothing harsh and nothing cruel in your whole rule; all your actions are dictated by clemency, courtesy, and humanity.'

[1] *ad Q.F.* i, 1, 25. For the other side of the picture see Arnold, *op. cit.* p. 80, and references.

Two points of the Roman system were especially praiseworthy. In the first place the Romans made no attempt to establish uniformity of government. Existing methods of taxation were taken over with slight adaptations. A municipal census had been regularly taken by the Greek cities of Asia Minor; it was kept up by the Romans down to the Civil War.[1] The judicial and financial arrangements established by Hiero in Sicily were taken over *en bloc*. In fact, wherever possible the Romans made use of the existing organisation of the country.

They were equally tolerant of local customs and religions. The Roman Pantheon was itself so eclectic that the governor had a very proper respect for the native deities. Cicero appeals to the Senate to punish the insults offered to the Sicilian shrines by Verres, 'for by regarding the religion of the allies, it would preserve its own faith'.[2] In later times Roman governors were not above associating themselves with the religious ceremonies in Egypt, and listening to the voice of the statue of Memnon.

Each province was organised as an entity, and co-operation between them was discouraged; but in accordance with the principle of flexibility the boundaries of the provinces were not sharply determined, especially in the East. Phrygia was sometimes attached to Asia, sometimes to Cilicia, according to the needs of the moment. In 56 three departments of it were placed under the governor of Cilicia, and the remainder under his colleague in Asia.[3] The position of Illyricum was similarly doubtful, and depended on the strategical

[1] Appian, *b.c.* v, 4.  [2] *II in Verr.* IV, 51, 114.
[3] v. Godt, *op. cit.* p. 19.

problem. Usually it seems to have gone with Macedonia, but it was joined with Cisalpine Gaul for Caesar.[1] The government of smaller areas could be changed with less ceremony. Münzer[2] deduces that M. Aemilius Lepidus, consul in 66, had Priene and Delos combined under his command about 80. As these islands were normally in different provinces, it follows that there must have been some elasticity in their administration.

Secondly, the Roman system allowed for a large measure of local autonomy. This was partly due to expediency, for there was no 'Lower Grade Civil Service' to take over the routine duties of administration; but an enlightened proconsul did cherish the fiction that the communities under his charge were 'free'. No doubt the Romans always favoured the aristocratic elements in the cities; the constitution granted by the Senate to Halaesa in 95 had a strongly aristocratic tinge.[3] But provided that a city's constitution met with the approval of Rome, it enjoyed considerable independence. Certain towns had special privileges; Tauromenium, for instance, was exempt from the duty of contributing towards naval defence. All the free and federate cities had the right of jurisdiction and maintained their own code of law. Cicero frankly tells a Roman business man, Decianus, that if he chooses to live in the free city of Apollonia he must abide by the local laws and accept their judgments.[4] The scrupulous respect usually shown to the rights of such communities is indicated by the fact

[1] That it was not an independent province is shown by Cicero's statement in 55 that if the two Gauls were made consular, Caesar would have no province left to him.

[2] *Römische Adelsparteien und Adelsfamilien*, p. 318.

[3] *II in Verr.* II, 49, 122.　　　[4] *pro Flacc.* 29, 70.

that when Lucullus wanted the franchise of Heraclea for his friend Archias, he could not requisition it, but had to ask for it as a favour.

Perhaps Rome's greatest gift to the provinces was the conception of justice which she introduced. As we have just said, Rome showed every consideration for the traditional sanctions which she found in force, but even the free towns would tend to adapt their own codes more or less to the *Lex provinciae* and the current edict. Cicero mentions it as a common practice for the free communities to adopt for themselves the laws which were passed at Rome.[1] It is to Rome's credit that she was on the whole so successful in reconciling local rights with Roman Law. The jurisdiction of the governor and of the towns existed side by side. Most of the minor civil cases would come before the local magistrate, and it was rarely that a governor exercised his latent power of over-riding the decision of the former. Cicero adjures his brother not to interfere in a complicated question of inheritance in Asia; 'for whoever heard of a praetor deciding that money was owed to so-and-so?'[2]

Important cases naturally came before the governor; and his jurisdiction was based on two principles. The first was that a case should if possible be tried on the spot, the second that the provincial should not be at a disadvantage before the Roman magistrate. Hence arose the system of assizes which took up so much of a governor's time. It was a special right of the Sicilians that no man should be ordered under forfeit to appear in a court outside his own district. Verres' flagrant disregard of this rule led to the famous consular decree of

[1] *pro Balb.* 8, 20.     [2] *ad Q.F.* I, 2, 10.

72, that no provincial should be tried in his absence on a capital charge. Moreover, if a question which concerned a provincial were brought up at Rome, it could be referred to the province for settlement. Thus, in 46, the urban praetor Volcatius Tullus referred a case of debt to the governor of Gaul because the debtor was resident there.[1]

In Sicily it was expressly ordained that in suits between a Roman and a Sicilian the judge should be of the same nationality as the defendant.[2] It says much for the goodwill which normally existed between the Roman and the provincial that the former should be willing to accept the judgments of the latter in certain circumstances. The Roman magistrates seem to have been equally impartial in their decisions. In the *senatus consultum* which gave freedom and immunity to Asclepiades for his services against the pirates, one clause allowed him the privilege of being tried either by the laws of his own country or before a Roman magistrate, as he preferred. If the Roman courts had had an unsavoury reputation, he would scarcely have been offered the choice. The integrity of the average governor is instanced by Flaccus' firm action in removing M. Caelius from his list of *recuperatores* or official arbitrators because of his flagrant determination to support his fellow-tax-gatherers under any circumstances.[3]

Finally, some attempt must be made to assess the financial position of the provincials. Stevenson[4] rightly admits that 'there is no reason to think that the republic imposed excessive financial burdens on its subjects'.

[1] *ad fam.* XIII, 14, 1.
[2] *II in Verr.* II, 13, 32.
[3] *pro Flacc.* 4, 11.
[4] *C.A.H.* IX, 471.

Livy tells us that the old system of taxation was main-tained in Macedonia, but the total amount of tribute demanded was exactly halved. Even in imperial times the theory was held that the taxes should merely defray the cost of military occupation.[1] In general, Rome at-tempted to equalise the burden of taxation throughout the province. Only a few privileged communities were granted exemption, while Roman citizenship itself had no great financial advantages. If a province was visited by foreign invasion the taxes were automatically lessened or remitted, and the contracts with the tax-farmers altered accordingly.[2] A slight but significant incident shows the favourable financial position of the provincials. The people of Caunia, a small town on the Aegean which had been 'attributed' by Sulla to Rhodes, petitioned the Senate that it might be allowed to pay taxes directly to it in future; although this would have meant the introduction of the Roman tax-gatherer.[3]

The personal extortions of a bad governor would affect only a handful of the wealthier natives. The pres-sure of the *publicani* was more widespread, but it is a mistake to regard the system of tax-farming as essen-tially vicious. In Sicily and Asia the *publicani* were responsible for the direct taxation; but in Sicily extortion was impossible if only the *Lex Hieronica* were obeyed, while in Asia the system was the only practicable method the Romans could have adopted. There was no existing political organisation which the Romans could make responsible for the collection of taxes; and the

[1] Tac. *hist.* IV, 74.
[2] *de leg. agr.* II, 30, 83; *de prov. cons.* 5, 12.
[3] *ad Q.F.* I, 1, 33.

produce which might have been paid to them as direct
tithe was unsuitable for Roman use. The tithe was a
direct tax, not a rent, and as such it replaced the heavy
land and municipal taxes of the Attalids. It was a re-
markably light impost at a time when bare land-rents
often ran as high as two-thirds of the produce.[1] The
Greeks of Asia might complain about the ubiquitous
tax-farmer; but when Sulla imposed a special five-year
impost upon the province as a war-indemnity, they were
compelled to call in the aid of the same system to raise
the money. In Cilicia and Bithynia the natives were
similarly obliged to invoke the help of the Roman
*publicani*. There were of course dangers in the system.
Not every governor had the strength of mind to stand
out against the financial interests as Lucullus did. But
the system *per se* certainly does not deserve all the ob-
loquy which has been attached to it.

*          *          *          *

It is incorrect to speak of the 'failure' of the senatorial administration of the provinces; for it continued as
a vigorous and on the whole efficient system as long as
the Senate maintained its power at Rome. It had its
weaknesses; the narrow prejudice against the extension
of the franchise, the lack of continuity and co-operation,
the absence of a supreme court of appeal at Rome. But as
long as a governor was willing to play his part, the
system worked as well as most institutions which have
been established by experiment rather than by theory.
The governor had a great responsibility. The Senate

[1] Cf. Tenney Frank, 'Dominium Soli', *J.R.S.* xvii; see also article
by Rostovtzeff in *C.A.H.* (viii) for previous taxation of Pergamum.

never attempted to interfere in strategy, and rarely in the internal administration of a province. It trusted in the man on the spot. To-day the tendency is towards centralisation, and no modern imperial power allows its governors such a free hand. But if the governor is circumscribed by too many restrictions, his authority is diminished and his judgment lacks decision.

The Senatorial System depended for its maintenance upon two conditions. In the first place it postulated a steady supply of men of the right material, experienced and loyal, who could handle absolute power without wishing to use it for their own ends; and secondly, it implied that the Senate should support the governor in return against the forces of disruption, the financial classes and others, in the province, and against his private enemies at home. The former condition was broken when ambitious generals seized provinces as stepping-stones to power, the latter by the gradual advance of the Equites. The selfishness of the self-styled 'popular' leaders led them to transgress the unwritten code of loyalty to the Senate. The unholy alliance of finance and politics at Rome allowed the Equites far too much influence in the provinces. Hence the time was ripe for that complete reform of the provincial system which was carried out by Caesar and Augustus. But they built upon the old senatorial foundations. The Roman Empire of the Caesars was not the new creation of a day, but a heritage direct from that much-maligned body, the Senate of Rome.

# BIBLIOGRAPHY

## (a) GENERAL

\*_The Cambridge Ancient History._ Vol. IX, 133–44 B.C. Cambridge, 1932.

\*Arnold, W. T. _The Roman System of Provincial Administration._ 1906.

\*Mommsen, Th. _Römisches Staatsrecht._ Leipzig, 1886–7.

\*Sands, P. C. _Client Princes of the Roman Empire._ Cambridge, 1907.

\*Jolliffe, R. O. _Phases of Corruption in Roman Administration._ Chicago, 1917.

\*Strassburger, H. _Concordia Ordinum._ Frankfort, 1932.

Frank, T. _Roman Imperialism._ New York, 1914.

Marsh, F. B. _Founding of the Roman Empire._ Oxford, 1926.

Rostovtzeff, M. _History of the Ancient World_, II: _Rome._ Oxford, 1927.

Holmes, T. Rice. _The Roman Republic._ Oxford, 1923.

Heitland, W. E. _The Roman Republic._ Cambridge, 1923.

Greenidge, A. H. J. _Roman Public Life._ London, 1911.

Petersson, T. _Cicero._ Berkeley, 1920.

Warde Fowler, W. _Social Life at Rome in the age of Cicero._ London, 1909.

Gelzer, M. _Die Nobilität der römischen Republik._ Leipzig, 1912.

Münzer, F. _Römische Adelsparteien und Adelsfamilien._ Stuttgart, 1920.

Stein, A. _Der römische Ritterstand._ Munich, 1927.

Godt, T. _Quomodo provinciae...administratae sint._ Kiel, 1876.

Tyrrell and Purser. _The Correspondence of Cicero._ v.d.

Meyer, E. _Caesars Monarchie._ Stuttgart, 1922.

Carcopino, J. *Sylla, ou la monarchie manquée*. Paris, 1931.

Willems, P. *Le Sénat de la République romaine*. Louvain, 1878–83.

Ferrero, G. *The Greatness and Decline of Rome* (trans.). London, 1907–8.

Kroll, W. *Die Kultur der ciceron. Zeit*. Leipzig, 1933.

Frank, T. *An Economic Survey of Ancient Rome*. Vol. I. Baltimore, 1933.

Marquardt, J. *Römische Staatsverwaltung*. Leipzig, 1881–5.

Drumann, W. *Geschichte Roms*. Revised by P. Groebe. Berlin, 1899.

Boak, A. E. R. 'The Extraordinary Commands', *Am. Hist. Rev.* 1918–19.

Hardy, E. G. 'The Number of the Sullan Senate', *J.R.S.* 1916.

Gelzer, M. 'Die römische Gesellschaft zur Zeit Ciceros', *N.J.* 1920.

Groebe, P. 'Die Obstruktion im römischen Senat', *Klio*, 1905.

Schur, W. 'Homo Novus', *Bonner Jahrb.* 1929.

Dessau, H. 'Gaius Rabirius Postumus', *Hermes*, 1911.

Frank, T. 'Dominium Soli', *J.R.S.* XVII; 'The Background of the Lex Manilia', *Class. Phil.* IX, 191.

(Also further articles referred to in footnotes.)

## (b) SPECIAL FOR LUCULLUS

Reinach, Th. *Mithridate Eupator*. Paris, 1890.

Drumann, W. *Geschichte Roms*. Revised by P. Groebe. Vol. IV. Leipzig.

Gelzer, M. 'Lucullus'† and other articles in Pauly-Wissowa's *Realencyclopädie*.

Dobiáš, J. 'Les premiers rapports des Romains avec les Parthes', *Archiv Orientalni*, III, 1931, 215.

† P.W. 13, 1: Licinius, Lucullus, no. 104.

Munro, J. A. R. 'Roads in Pontus', *J.H.S.* xxi, 1901, 52.

Eckhardt, K. 'Die armenischen Feldzüge des Lucullus', *Klio*, ix–x, 1909–10.

Guse, F. 'Die Feldzüge des dritten Mithridatischen Krieges', *Klio*, xx, 1926, 332.

Holmes, T. Rice. *Op. cit.* i, 409–26.

Especial acknowledgment is due to the authors of the works marked with an asterisk in the above list. (J. M. C.)

# INDEX

Roman citizens are cited under the names by which they are most commonly known. The year of their tenure of the consulship (cos.) or other important office is inserted for purposes of identification. Laws are grouped under the heading of *lex*: the date is given in brackets where possible.

Achaia, 36, 58, 94, 153, 161, 163

Acilius Glabrio, M'. (cos. 67), 114, 122 ff.

Adherbal, 61

Adramyttene, 175

*aedilicium vectigal*, 189, 194

Aedui, the, 41, 63, 175

Aemilius Lepidus, M. (cos. 66), 202

— Paullus, L. (cos. 50), 73

— Scaurus, M. (praet. 56), 149

Africa, province of, 46, 55, 103, 167

Albinus, 18

Albucius, T. (praet. 105), 147

Alexandria, 62, 68, 175

Allobroges, the, 36 f., 63, 164

Amisus, 113, 116

Antioch, 47

Antiochus of Commagene, 16, 176

Antonius, C. (cos. 63), 35

— M. (cos. 99), 43

— — (cos. 44), 143

— Creticus, M. (praet. 75), 44, 49, 75, 90, 107

— Hybrida, C. (cos. 63), 74

Aquilius, M'. (cos. 129), 26

— — (cos. 101), 159, 161, 167f.

Archias, 203

Ariobarzanes I of Cappadocia, 58, 61

— III, 61 f., 152

Ariovistus, 16, 63, 93, 159

Armenia, 122, 135

Armies: of Caesar, 92, 178f.; of Cicero, 179, 191; of Crassus, 96, 179; of Lucullus, 113 ff., 132 ff., 180 f.; of Pompey, 96, 179

Army, the Roman, 53, 178 ff.

Arverni, the, 63

Asclepiades, 34, 204

Asia, province of, 38, 45 ff., 56, 82, 101, 110 ff., 138, 160 ff., 169, 179, 192, 195 ff.; taxation of, 23, 27, 128, 195, 205

Assembly, the, and the Senate, 12 ff., 19, 90 f., 93, 122

*assessores*, 140, 152

Ateius Capito, C. (trib. 55), 53

Attalus III of Pergamum, 13, 65

Atticus, T. Pomponius, 141

Augustus, the emperor, 62, 207

Aurelius Cotta, C. (cos. 75), 11, 33, 105

— — L. (cos. 65), 33, 86

— — M. (cos. 74), 33, 75, 103, 110 ff., 151

Auxiliary troops, 68, 182

Balearic Isles, the, 46

Bibulus, M. Calpurnius (cos. 59), 32, 36, 69, 81, 86, 147, 151, 158, 160, 162, 182

Bithynia, bequest of, 27, 65, 108 ff.; province of, 62, 82, 110 ff., 120 ff., 161; taxation of, 29, 206

*boni*, 11, 34

Brogitarus, 17

Brutus, M. Junius (praet. 44), 156, 174, 191 n.

Byzantines, the, 143

Cabira, 113

Caelius Caldus, C., quaestor in Cilicia, 81, 144, 155

Caelius, M. (trib. 52), 7, 24, 40, 77

Caesar, C. Julius (cos. 59), *pontifex maximus*, 35, 52; governor of Farther Spain, 81, 155, 193, 198; consulate of, 7, 14 f., 32 f., 36, 68, 92, 157 f., 171; in Gaul, 41, 63, 75, 95, 141, 146, 159, 177 ff., 199; expedition to Britain, 47; recall of, 5, 77, 85, 98, 146; at Alexandria, 62; and Egypt, 67, 70, 91; and the Transpadanes, 121, 165; and the provinces, 77, 84, 86; and the client-princes, 16, 61; and Pompey, 16, 51, 68, 128; and the Senate, 19, 37, 50, 56, 61, 92, 148, 151, 170; and the Equites, 23, 24; aims of, 9, 54, 59, 63, 134

— L. Julius (cos. 64), 86

Calidius, Cn., 46

Cappadocia, 58, 62, 164

Cassiterides, the, 47

Cassius Longinus, C. (trib. 49), 73, 82

Catilina, L. Sergius (praet. 68), 21, 34 ff., 49

Cato, M. Porcius (praet. 54), 5 n., 6 f., 15, 22 f., 37, 51 f., 73, 79, 86, 95, 137, 146 f.; mission to Cyprus, 17, 32, 145, 158, 164, 167; character of, 31

Catulus, Q. Lutatius (cos. 78), 11, 15, 18, 34 ff., 50, 52, 66, 68, 75, 88, 103, 124, 127

Caunia, 205

Cethegus, P. Cornelius (trib. 74), 105, 110

Chalcedon, 113

Cicero, M. Tullius (cos. 63), consulate of, 74, 170; banishment and recall of, 24, 28, 31, 34, 37, 154, 173; in Cilicia, 30, 33, 40, 61, 76, 80 f., 86, 138, 194, chapters v and vi *passim*; and Appius, 78; and the *publicani*, 29; and the Equites, 20 ff., 28; and the Senate, 2, 10, 36, 147; and Pompey, 37, 50 f., 94, 128, 142, 192 f.; and the provinces, 30, 39, 149, 164; character of, 30, 40; value of, as evidence, 186, 192

— Q. Tullius, governor of Asia, 29, 45, 77, 80, 138, 141, 152, 156, 175 f., 184, 200

Cilicia, province of, 27, 37, 43, 75 ff., 82, 93, 110, 115, 117, 126, 129, 146, 160, 170, 179 f., 187, 206 (*see also* Cicero)

Cineas, 30

Claudius Pulcher, Appius (cos. 79), 193

— — — (cos. 54), 82; governor of Cilicia, 62, 74, 78, 80 f., 154, 168, 191, 194

Client-kingdoms, 58 ff., 136, 177; annexation of, 64 ff.

Clodius, P. (trib. 58), 6, 17, 31 n., 32, 55 f., 64, 140 f., 153, 164,

Clodius—*cont.*
167, 171, 173; intrigues of, in
Asia, 114ff., 178
Cnidus, 175
*coloniae*, 26, 46, 177, 187
*comites*, 139f.
Commercial interests, 42ff.
Commissions of organisation, 114,
121, 130, 141, 168ff.
*concordia ordinum*, 20, 24
Conscription, 179
Cornelius, C. (trib. 67), legisla-
tion of, 5 n., 13, 21, 36, 55, 174
Cornificius, Q. (quaest. 48), 170
Corn supply, the, 55, 94, 123
Corruption at Rome, 16f., 22, 59,
66, 150, 173f.
Cosconius, C. (praet. 89), 77
Crassus, M. Licinius (cos. 70), in
the Servile War, 90; censorship
of, 35; and the Equites, 23, 28;
and Egypt, 27, 50, 68f.; and
Pompey, 49, 52, 68, 90, 95, 128;
Parthian expedition of, 47, 53,
58, 69, 75, 82, 96, 146, 159
Crete, 36, 49, 174
Curio, C. Scribonius (cos. 76), 11,
126, 147
— — — (trib. 50), 5, 17, 48, 50
*cursus honorum*, 1, 143
Cyprus, 17, 32, 56, 64, 164, 189
Cyrene, bequest of, 64f.; province
of, 145

Danala, 130
Dardanus, Treaty of, 48, 101
Defence, problem of, 176ff.
Deiotarus, tetrarch of Galatia, 17,
61, 174, 182
Delos, 43, 45f., 202
Dion, 176

*dispensationes*, 14
Diviciacus, 175
Dolabella, Cn. Cornelius (cos. 81),
147, 149
Domitius Ahenobarbus, L. (cos.
54), 74, 82, 87
— Calvinus, Cn. (cos. 53), 82
Drusus, M. Livius (trib. 91), 15, 26
Dyrrhachium, 188

*edictum tralaticium*, 161
Egypt, bequest of, 65
Egyptian question, the, 27, 50ff.,
63, 66ff., 91, 96, 159, 167, 173
Embassies, from Rome, 166ff.; to
Rome, 172ff.
*encomia*, 176
Equites, the, and the Senate, 2,
19ff., 119, 148; and Pompey,
118ff., 126ff.; aims of, 53; influence of, 25ff., 57, 59, 115,
128, 132f., 207
Extortion in the provinces, 42,
184, 188ff.
Extraordinary commands, 59, 72,
87ff., 124ff., 141

Fabius Maximus Allobrogicus, Q.
(cos. 121), 164
— Sanga, 164
Fimbria, C. Flavius, 48, 100, 180
*Fimbriani*, the, 114ff., 122, 133,
178, 180
Financial organisation, 56, 139,
144, 154ff., 181, 187, 197
Flaccus, L. Valerius (cos. 86), 48,
122, 180
— — — (praet. 63), 149, 184, 204
Fonteius, M., 77

Gabinius, A. (cos. 58), tribunate
of, 13, 21, 36, 55, 122ff., 133,
174; legate of Pompey, 141;

Gabinius—*cont.*
  consulate of, 27; governor of Syria, 28, 34, 41, 56, 80, 93, 97, 141, 146f., 177; misgovernment of, 97, 151, 188; expedition to Egypt, 61, 69, 94, 151, 160; trial of, 28, 69
Gades, 34, 193
Gaditani, the, 18
Gaetuli, the, 164
Galatia, 182
Gaul, 41, 46f., 58, 63, 75, 86, 144, 166, 170
— Cisalpine, 14, 109, 164, 179
— Transalpine, 77, 92, 164
Genetiva Julia, 165
Gordyene, 167
Gracchus, C. Sempronius (trib. 123), 13, 20, 25, 48, 71
— T. Sempronius (trib. 133), 13, 39, 65

Halaesa, 202
Helvetii, the, 41
Heraclea, 113, 203
Herod the Great, 61
Hirrus, C. Lucilius, 7
Hortensius, Q. (cos. 69), 11, 35f., 66, 68, 76, 124, 127

Illyricum, 77, 177, 201
Imperialism, 52 ff., 66, 119, 129
*imperium*, 62, 72, 77, 80, 83, 93, 114, 125, 127, 129, 141
Isauria, 180

Juba, King of Numidia, 48
Judaea, 27
Jugurtha, 26, 53
Juncus, M., 110, 146
Jurisdiction in the provinces, 203 ff.

Lamia, L. Aelius, 28
Lampsacus, 163
Laterensis, 24
*legati*, 81, 94, 124f., 140ff.
*legatio libera*, 167, 170f.
Lentulus Marcellinus, governor of Cyrene, 145
— P. Cornelius, quaestor in Asia, 82
— Spinther, P. Cornelius (cos. 57), 29, 33, 37, 68, 75, 77, 126, 146f., 159, 193
Lepidus, M. Aemilius (cos. 78), 18, 34, 75, 88, 103
*Lex curiata de imperio*, 77ff., 83
— *provinciae*, 161ff., 169, 203
*Lex, leges: Aebutia*, 141; *Aurelia* (70), 20; *Corneliae* (81) *de maiestate*, 158, 194, *de provinciis ordinandis*, 72, 78; *Cornelia* (67) '*ut praetores*', 162; *Gabinia* (67), 35f., 44, 49, 91, 123ff., 141, *de legationibus*, 172; *Hieronica* (of Sicily), 153, 168; *Julia de repetundis* (59), 96, 148, 157f., 168, 171, 194; *Licinia*, 141; *Mamilia* (110), 26; *Manilia* (66), 21, 34ff., 44f., 49, 51, 56, 91, 127ff., 170; *Plotia de vi* (78), 34; *Pompeia de iuribus magistratuum* (52), 83; *Pupia*, 172; *Roscia* (67), 21, 24, 126; *Sempronia de provinciis* (123), 71; *Sulpicia* (88), 72; *Terentia Cassia* (73), 55; *de Termessibus* (70), 19, 153; *Trebonia* (55), 95; *Vatinia de Caesaris provincia* (59), 92; *Villia annalis* (180), 102
Lilybaeum, 144
Lucca, conference of, 52, 69, 95
Lucullus, L. Licinius (cos. 74),

Lucullus—*cont.*

    early career of, 100 ff., 168, 183, 189; and Sulla, 100, 102, 117; consulate of, 33, 75, 103 ff.; command of, in the East, 76, 107 ff., 146; and Mithridates, 112 ff.; settlement of Asia, 113, 118, 136, 195 ff.; recall of, 27, 51, 53, 98, 115 ff.; triumph of, 51, 134; closing years of, 134 f.; and Pompey, 51, 80, chapter IV *passim*; and Caesar, 136; and the Senate, 11, 41, 132 f., 150, 169; aims of, 53 n., 58, 135 ff.; character of, 113, 117, 128, 132, 135 ff.; importance of, 99

— M. Licinius (cos. 73), 11, 33, 35, 100, 102, 106, 147, 169

Lycia, 59

Macedonia, province of, 28 f., 35 f., 56, 59, 76, 82, 93, 95, 106, 145 f., 155, 174, 177, 179; taxation of, 205

Magnesia, 176

Manilius, C. (trib. 66), 127

Manlius, C., 71

Marcellus, C. Claudius (cos. 50), 33, 48

— M. Claudius (cos. 51), 33, 83, 98 n.

Marcius Rex, Q. (cos. 68), 51, 117, 120 ff.

Marius, C. (cos. 107), 13, 26, 43, 72, 87, 156, 164, 178

Masinissa, King of Numidia, 61

Meniscus, 34

Messius, C. (trib. 56), 95

Metelli, the, 38, 52, 100

Metellus, L. Caecilius (cos. 68), 152

Metellus, M. Caec. (praet. 69), 11

— Balearicus, Q. Caec. (cos. 123), 46

— Celer, Q. Caec. (cos. 60), 16, 23, 74, 92

— Creticus, Q. Caec. (cos. 69), 36, 49, 51, 91

— Nepos, Q. Caec. (cos. 57), 95, 157, 179

— Pius, Q. Caec. (cos. 80), 31, 33, 75, 89, 111, 160

Miletus, 184

Minucius Thermus, Q., 81, 102

Mithridates VI Eupator, 48, 53, 58, 60, chapter IV *passim*, 159, 181 f.

Mithridatic War, First, 100, 168, 179, 196

— — Second, 101

— — Third, 27, chapter IV *passim*, 183

Mitylene, 101

Mucius Scaevola, Q. (cos. 95), 29, 154, 161, 192

*municipia*, 187

Murena, L. Licinius (praet. 88), 77, 101, 159

— — — (cos. 63), 29, 40, 73, 79, 131 n., 140, 150, 169

Mylasa, 175

Narbo Martius, 26, 177

Navy, the Roman, 41, 183 ff.

*negotiatores*, 45 f., 101, 196

Nicaea, 46

Nicomedes III of Bithynia, 65, 107, 159, 168

*nobiles*, 9

Novum Comum, 92, 163

*novus homo*, 10

Numidia, 17, 48, 72

Octavius, L. (cos. 75), 44, 110
— — officer of Pompey, 49
Optimates, the, 10, 35
*ornatio provinciae*, 94, 154 ff.
Oropus, 35, 175

Paphlagonia, 58
Papirius and Plautius (tribb. 89), 27
Parthia, 41, 47, 53, 54, 58, 74, 75, 96, 135, 150, 159 f.
Patronage, 163 ff.
*pauci*, 11
People, the Roman, aims of, 53, 59, 67, 127; power of, 71 f., 87
Pergamum, 65
Petra, 47
Petreius, M., 32
Pharnaces II, King of Bosporus, 61
Philippus, L. Marcius (cos. 91), 15, 88
Phraates III, King of Parthia, 54
Phrygia, 26, 48, 169, 201
Pinnius, 46
Piracy, 34, 43, 55, 106, 123, 126, 151, 183
Pirustae, the, 177
Piso, C. Calpurnius (cos. 67), 36
— Cn. Calp., 49
— L. Calp. (cos. 58), 27 f., 34, 41, 93, 190, chapters v and vi *passim*
Plancius, C. (trib. 56), 144
Polystratus, 34
Pompeius, Cn. Magnus (cos. 70), early commands of, 88, 104, 160; and the pirates, 49; eastern settlement of, 19, 27, 47, 51, 54, 61, 193, 199; and the Egyptian question, 69; and the corn-supply, 94, 97; Spanish command of, 79, 95; as sole consul, 83; and Caesar, 16, 51, 68, 92;

and Crassus, 49, 52, 68, 90, 95, 128; and Lucullus, 51, 80, chapter iv *passim*; and Cicero, 37, 50 f., 94, 128, 142, 192 f.; and the Senate, 37, 39, 56, 73, 104, 152, 170, 181; and the Equites, 21, 24 f., 28, 118 ff., 126 ff.; aims of, 54, 95, 123, 135 f.; character of, 51, 70, 117, 130, 149; achievements of, 87, 183, 189
— Strabo, Cn. (cos. 89), 188
Pomptinus, C. (praet. 63), 37, 78, 147
Pontus, province of, 114 f., 120 ff.
Populares, the, 10
Praecia, 110
*praefecti*, 145 n.
*prorogatio*, 71
Provinces, administration of the, 138 ff.
Provincial governor, appointment of, 71 ff.; duration of command of, 76 f.; installation of, 79 ff.; powers of, 138 ff., 165
Provincials, advantages of the, 192 ff., 199 ff.
Ptolemy X Alexander, King of Egypt, 67
— XI Auletes, King of Egypt, 16, 34, 66 ff., 159
— Apion, King of Cyrene, 65
— Neoteros, King of Cyrene, 64
— King of Cyprus, 64, 66
*publicani*, 25 f., 28 f., 59, 205 f.
Pupius Piso, M. (cos. 61), 74

*quaestiones*, 148
Quaestor, the, 81 f., 124, 143 ff., 156
Quinctius, L. (trib. 74), 105, 120

Rabirius Postumus, C., 69f.

*recuperatores*, 204

Rhegium, 159

Rhodes, 41

Roscius Otho, L. (trib. 67), 21

Roscius, Sextus, 11 n.

Rullus, P. Servilius (trib. 63), agrarian proposals of, 27, 68, 78, 91, 142

Rupilius, P. (cos. 132), 169

Rutilius Rufus, P. (cos. 105), 26, 51, 149


Salluvius Naso, C., 125

Sardinia, province of, 55, 147, 167

Scaptius, M., 191

Scipio Aemilianus, P. Cornelius (cos. 147), 10

— Africanus, P. Corn. (cos. 205), 87, 89

— Nasica, P. Corn. (cos. 138), 169

Senate, the, restoration of, 1 ff.; procedure in, 4 ff.; attendance in, 5 f.; parties in, 8 ff.; scope of, 12, 172; powers of, 18 f., 170; personnel of, 30 ff.; foreign policy of, chapter II *passim*; and the Assembly, 12 ff.; and the magistrates, 15 ff.; and the Equites, 19 ff., 119 ff., 132, 207; and Caesar, 92 f., 148; and the client-kings, 60 ff.; and the provincial appointments, 71 ff.; and the extraordinary commands, 88 ff., 97, 124 f.; and the provincial governors, 139, 146 ff., 194; weaknesses of the system, 59 f., 206 f.

Sentius Saturninus, C., 76

Sertorius, Q., in Spain, 104, 179; and Mithridates, 60

Servilius Isauricus Vatia, P. (cos. 79), 34, 44, 51, 76, 126, 180, 193

— Vatia, P. (cos. 48), 37 f., 79

Sestius, P. (trib. 57), 145, 193

'Ship-money', 183

Sicily, province of, 39, 46, 55, 59, 143, 150, 153, 161, 169, 175, 201, 203 f.; taxation of, 28, 152, 168, 201, 205

Sinope, 113

Sittius, P., 46, 50

Sophene, 167

Spain, 46, 56, 79, 89, 95, 157, 164, 199; taxation of, 193

— Farther, 198.

— Hither, 49, 89, 95

Staienus (quaest. 77), 17

Sulla, L. Cornelius, and Mithridates, 48, 58, 60, 61; aims of, 1 ff., 72, 76; reforms of, 1, 13, 20, 72, 75, 176; and the Egyptian question, 66; and Lucullus, 100 ff.; and Pompey, 88, 103; death of, 102

Sulpicius Rufus, Servius (cos. 51), 73, 181

*supplicatio*, 41, 50, 146

Syracuse, 176, 190

Syria, province of, 28, 47, 58, 82, 86, 93, 95, 135, 146, 160, 182; taxation of, 27 f., 176

Syro-Cilicia, 128


Tadius, P., 143

Tauromenium, 190, 202

Tax-farming, 28, 35, 128, 190, 195 ff., 205 f.

Tenedos, 150, 165, 176

Teutones, the, 63

Tiberius, the emperor, 77

Tigranes I of Armenia, 61, 113 f., 133, 167

Tigranocerta, 113, 119, 182

Transpadanes, the, 121, 165, 182

Trebatius Testa, C., 47, 140

Trebonius, C. (cos. 45), 82, 95

Tribunate, the, restoration of, 13, 83, 105; misuse of, 7, 16, 120

*tribuni aerarii*, 149

Triumphs, award of, 37, 51, 79, 121, 134, 146 ff.

Triumvirate, the First, 11, 28, 32, 37, 52, 54, 59, 95

Tyrians, the, 176

Vaccaei, the, 159

Valerius Messala, M. (cos. 53), 82

Vatinius, P. (cos. suff. 47), 14, 16, 73, 92, 141 f., 167

Veneti, the, 166

Vergilius, C., governor of Sicily, 31

—— legate of Piso, 143

Verres, C. (praet. 74), quaestor in Gaul, 144; legate in Cilicia, 140, 142, 160; governor of Sicily, 77, 80, 190, chapters v and vi *passim*; trial of, 6, 34 ff., 44, 149, 186 n.

Vienne, 199

Volcatius Tullus (praet. 46), 204

Xenocles of Adramyttene, 175